NO WAY OUT

Lee Flandreau

Hardback
International Standard Book Number: 978-1-60452-184-9
Softback
International Standard Book Number: 978-1-60452-185-6
eBook
International Standard Book Number: 978-1-60452-186-3

Library of Congress Control Number: 2022932988

BluewaterPress LLC
2922 Bella Flore Ter
New Smyrna Beach FL 32168

This book may be purchased online at -
https://www.bluewaterpress.com

Foreword

*N*o *Way Out* is a true story of an unusual exploit. It begins when two men from Chicago— one of whom is my unafraid and unabashed grandfather—discover a mutual fascination for the Amazon Rainforest. Its jungle, much of it unexplored, its thousands of animal species, both known and unknown, the lush and boundless vegetation, the natives who dwelled within: it was all so overwhelming, different, enticing. So they went. Embarking upon what seemed like a highly detailed and careful plan, the duo set out for eastern Peru to the very remote town of Puerto Maldonado, where they cruised down the Tombopata and Madre de Dios rivers toward Bolivia. Gradually, their meticulous plans dissolved, raising earnest concerns and a mounting sense of entrapment.

While they clung to their sense of humor amidst sheer turmoil, their frustration mounted, resulting in a tale that I feel so honored to share. This saga of the Amazon should be a must-read for those looking to venture into a foreign corner of the globe where their hearts are presumed to be, but their very own language cannot be found.

Kelly McCarthy
Creative writer
and strategist
Los Angeles

Edited by Carole J. Greene

Chapter 1

Four Thousand Miles Due South

Eastern Airlines flight 17 to Lima, Peru, rattled and roared down the runway of the Miami International Airport and instantly became quiet as it lifted to airborne, sucking in its landing gear with a thump. Bill Lutz and I sat back, quietly celebrating our good fortune of sitting in coach class and having an empty seat between us. Bill could unwind that 6'4" frame and we could both have elbowroom, a luxury on any flight. This trip was going to take about six hours.

It was May 23, 1990, springtime in America, autumn where we were going, and we were off to a place neither of us had ever been, with luggage we had never used, packed with things we had never taken on vacations or business trips. We were gaining altitude over Biscayne Bay and still had some daylight left for looking out the window.

In the next few minutes, Bill acted like he was going to sleep so I punched him and asked, "Lutzy, have you ever seen Cuba? Look out your window!" We were still low enough to see the sparse Cuban countryside, small houses and a few dusty old cars on the road. Cuba had not boomed in the thirty-plus years of Castro's promises and marathon speeches. It looked very much like the Russian countryside I had once seen from the air.

Bill gave it a, "Yuck, not much."

I turned to my adventuresome partner again. "You realize you are going to be Guillermo on this trip, don't you?

"Why's that?"

"Because that's Spanish for William." I wrote it out for him. "It is pronounced Gee-yare-mo." He looked at it, smiled and practiced it a few times. He seemed to like it. I guessed that after being called plain old monosyllabic "Bill" all his life, same as those damn things we get in the mail almost daily, he might enjoy the change. I called him nothing but Guillermo for the rest of the trip except for some x-rated words when he deserved them or in retaliation for the ones he called me.

Two hours earlier, Bill and I had met at the Eastern Airlines ticket counter in this tangle of confused humanity they called Miami International Airport. It was like a giant humidor with the mixed aromas of jet engine and bus exhaust accented with a whiff of sweat and a pinch of refried beans. Miami is probably the only airport in the country where the second language was Ingles. Bill had come from his home in Riverwoods, a northern suburb of Chicago. I had flown in by a small commercial flight from my place in Naples, Florida. We were busy talking about the weird things in our luggage while we waited patiently at the ticket counter. Ahead of us was a tall, animated, fast-talking brunette chattering in Spanish and tying up two agents at the same time.

"What's her problem?"

"No idea, I can't catch anything they are saying. Spanish has a lot more syllables to say the same thing in English. She just sounds like a machine gun."

Her problem was finally solved; we checked in and watched our two large duffel bags disappear down the belt, wondering how they would arrive in Peru.

Bill snarled, "What a zoo this is. All these little people going around speaking Spanish, weird bags, you'd think we were already in Peru."

"Yep, this is the most popular airport in this country for Latin America. Our own business associates from Mexico and all points south will come here a lot more easily than going up to Chicago. That is why we put our Latin American office for International here."

This was 1990, more than twenty years before the invention of the iPhone and the 21st century addiction to cell phones—those forgotten days before public places were filled with zombies who walked around with both hands on a tablet, typing with their thumbs, or people with earplug phones that annoy everyone by talking out loud while looking glassy-eyed out into space. It was also before the 9/11 attack and the exhaustive TSA pre-boarding security checks that resulted and will be with us forever. There was no need to be x-rayed, patted down or to put yourself back together afterward by putting your shoes and belts on, reloading your pockets or saying goodbye to that tiny pocket knife that was taken from you.

We had a couple of hours to kill before our flight—and the Miami International Airport was not a great place to hang out—but I had retained my membership in the American Airlines' Admirals Club from my business traveling days. They were welcome oases in any airport, with comfortable seating, TV, snacks and a bar.

Even though we were flying on Eastern, no matter where we decided to wait in this airport, there would still be a marathon walk to the gate. The Admirals Club would at least give us a chance to sit comfortably, have a snack and a drink and talk about this questionable trip we were about to take—discuss it in person, for a change, instead of on the phone.

When we reached the lounge and stood at the desk to have an I.D. check, not one person there could miss noticing in the lounge area beyond, the same brunette who was raising hell at the check-in counter ahead of us was stretched across an entire sofa, reading, with both feet up on the arm, displaying a perfect pair of long, tan, well curved legs.

"Damn, that is some real eye candy there." Another old gawker at the counter announced.

The woman at the desk caught us looking. "Aha, that ees Gabriela Sabatini, tennis player of Argentina." I knew I recognized those legs. Well, they must have done more than decorate lounges that year; she won the U. S. Open later in the year, and she had to beat Steffi Graf to do it. Those were tough odds, but probably better odds than our odds of seeing a comparable pair of legs on this trip.

We utilized our waiting time to look over our itinerary and double-check our immediate plans after our arrival in Lima. We were going to arrive late and had an early flight to Cuzco. We had booked a hotel in Lima for one night to catch a few winks before going on to Cuzco the next day on a Peruvian airline. After a delay in Cuzco, we would go on over the Andes range and down the eastern slope to our final destination in some remote part of the Amazon valley rainforest.

This flight so far had been smooth. I learned long ago that air turbulence was activated by the travel gods only when food or drinks were being served. The sun was setting at about the time we passed over Panama and then the coastline of South America. Rising abruptly beyond the coast was the massive Andes mountain range. Once we'd passed the sprinkle of lights from the high-altitude cities in the mountains, the ground was completely dark. It meant we had probably crossed the equator and were over the sprawling jungles of Amazonia.

The flight attendant put down our trays and, with a smile and a "voila," ceremoniously peeled back the aluminum foil covering our Eastern Airlines banquet. This evening they were featuring an easily forgettable reheated meat, mashed potatoes and, of course, peas. Afterward, we tried to kick back and catch a wink before landing, but our pumped-up anticipation kept thoughts slapping around in our empty heads.

I pulled out my small Spanish dictionary and did a little practicing, since I was to be the designated communicator. My long forgotten two years of Spanish in high school were under the instruction of Señorita Mudge. Yes, "Mudge;" there are lots of Germans in Cincinnati. Then, I had two years of Spanish at college, the minimum requirement for an AB degree, instructed by Señor Berrios, who talked so fast they called him the Puerto Rican machine gun. He and Señorita Mudge could never have chatted.

I knew a lot of words but could never handle a high-speed conversation. Traveling in Latin America for business during the past years, I had always been accompanied by our Vice President for Latin America, Manolo de la Torriente, and had ignored my own conversational skills. Manolo, a Cuban-born American, spoke a high-class Spanish and was a skilled businessman.

Manolo taught me to excuse myself by saying that I do know some Spanish words but can't converse by saying, "Yo comprendo muchas palabras, pero no puedo hablar." The only problem with that was that the better I learned to say that, the more I sounded like I did speak Spanish. They just look at you and say, "Aha, esta hablando" (aha, you are speaking) and they don't get it. Better to just say, "Pocito," and shake your head.

It had become clear during the planning of this trip that our guide and his crew really spoke no English—one of the many challenges awaiting us. Bill's Spanish was interesting. He would simply tack an "o" on the end of an English word. "Whereo iso the toileto?" One time, in haste, he tacked an "o" on the word "no." That was a beauty, "no-o." Good for some smiles but also amazing when it worked.

We were to land in Lima at about 10:00 pm. We had a room booked at the Jose Antonio Hotel, hoping to catch some zzz's before our flight to Cuzco in the morning, then continuing on to our final destination to the small, isolated jungle town of Puerto Maldonado, on the banks of the Tambopata River in the extreme southeast area of Peru's Amazon rainforest. It is about 100 miles, as the crow flies, from the Bolivian border.

This was to be our base city. We would travel from there with our guide, Victor, and his "staff," Jose, in his powered riverboat. We were to stay our first night at a government-owned hotel called Hotel de Turistas, which had been self-rated as a Three Star hotel. Food and other provisions for the trip would be discussed and determined when we arrived, and then we would provide the funds. From Puerto Maldonado we would leave for our cruise through the jungle, down the river, and return there in a couple of weeks.

Chapter 2

Hatching this Plan

The genesis of this curious trip was after a golf game at the Thorngate Country Club in Deerfield, Illinois. It was a game that was great for Bill Lutz but disastrous for me. I had not only lost at a dice game and had to buy breakfast for twenty grinning guys in the dining room but then my partner, Warty, and I were soundly trounced by our opponents, Lutz and Allen, in the match when Bill Lutz hit his second shot into the hole on a par five for a nearly impossible "double eagle." It was the first one any of us had ever seen and about a thousand times harder to shoot than a hole-in-one. It is also called an "Albatross." Three under par on one hole. You can do that only with a two on a par five or a hole in one on a par four. It was the first Albatross ever shot at the Thorngate Country Club.

I was sitting in the locker room bar afterward, a place known as "The Cave," a cigar smoke-filled den next to the men's locker room, where gin rummy is played and the sounds ranged from quiet laughs to loud profanity. I sat with my opponent, Bill

Lutz, sipping my free drink (tradition forced him to buy) and lamented my empty wallet. I had to watch Bill get his high-fives all afternoon as others finished their rounds and heard the news. His scorecard was permanently mounted.

Bill had a successful business of his own in Northern Illinois and he knew that I was in charge of the international operations for Signode Corporation and that I traveled overseas about half the time. During a break, in between his collecting handshakes and "attaboys," Bill turned to me and said, "Lipper, I guess you've been about everywhere in the world? How long have you been traveling overseas?"

(Note: Bill seldom, if ever, called anyone by his real name. The full list of addresses he uses include things like Hammer, Ham, Liplock, Lips, Lipper, Cocker, Bunky, Big Boy and Hunyak, none of which have ever been defined, or bear any resemblance to anything or anyone, living or dead.)

I took a long sip of my brew, did some quick math and responded, "Sixteen years—ever since I moved back here from Canada. Oh, and the two months I spent in Germany and South Africa in 1970 before that. But, to answer the first part of your question, the answer is no, I have not been everywhere. Mostly I visit the largest operations, the ones where we manufacture, located in the major industrialized countries. I haven't spent time in the communist, eastern bloc countries or in the smaller, undeveloped areas like parts of Africa, Russia or the Middle East. We had begun in India and I had a few meetings with the government in China. But...what I would really like to do someday is go to the Amazon. That enormous rainforest has some of the world's secrets in it, those thousands of unknown species, huge fish in the rivers, jaguars, the jungle, monkeys, poisonous frogs, tapirs, anacondas, the longest snakes in the world and fish we don't have anywhere else...."

Bill jumped. "Me too! I've always wanted to do that!" he spurted. "Let's do it!

"I want to go there. Maybe we can catch some of those giant catfish and explore the jungle. Maybe shoot some birds? I've always had the same idea. Let's do it!"

Now that was probably the first sign that we both had loose screws somewhere. A pair of half brains with the same idea could be dangerous. I thought for a moment that Bill was just pumped up with his "albatross" adrenaline rush, but we agreed to each research different trips and get back together later. For now and the rest of that day, he had to deal with his instant celebrity.

Would he get smashed and forget what we agreed to do? No way. Bill doesn't drink.

In the next few weeks I began seriously looking at Amazon trips with a travel agent I had used for years. The cruises with ocean-going vessels that steam into the mouth of the Amazon from the Atlantic Ocean and up the wide river to the city of Manaus were available but would probably be like going into a lake, landing in the only real civilized port in the entire Amazon Valley. That would not be a jungle tour. We wanted to see some nature—some jungle, trees, birds, fish, and native people.

The closest thing I found was a smaller boat cruise from Iquitos, Peru, on the upper end of the Amazon, just on the eastern slope of the Andes. From there the river flowed toward the confluence with the black water of the Rio Negro at that same city of Manaus. As a final destination, Manaus seemed to be ideal. It had been a boom town during the great growth of the rubber business in the late nineteenth century and early twentieth and offered a large island of civilization in this vast jungle, with nice hotels, an ornate, historic opera house, maybe even flights to get us home.

Iquitos too had a history during the rubber boom, a time when the only real exploration of the vast rainforest began. It had ended in about 1920 when the seeds of rubber trees that had been taken out years earlier and planted on easily accessible farms in Indonesia and Malaysia began to produce.

My Iquitos trip would be a very long one, however, but we could see the wildlife and trees plus get a feel for the Amazon. It was over 900 boat miles, which was probably too long. It might mean steaming day and night without many stops. Also, the river downstream seemed less interesting. It is a wide expanse of water, miles across, like a slowly moving lake, not a jungle full of plants and animals that we wanted to see.

Bill, in his search, ran across an ad in some adventure magazine that read:

Guide Service

Puerto Maldonado, Peru

Field Research

Explore this unique jungle with Barbara Fearis, wildlife photographer and birdwatcher from San Francisco, California

Bill contacted Fearis by phone early in 1990 and received two handwritten pages with her Guide license copied in the middle of the page. It declared that Barbara Gianferante Fearis was a "Guia Practico de Turismo" in the Republic of Peru. She suggested a couple of places we could visit and suggested that we wait until the rainy season subsided in late March. Bill replied that he would have an opportunity to visit California for a convention in late February and would like to meet and discuss it further.

During his business visit in February he met her for lunch in Sausalito. Fearis was fifty-two years old, billed herself as a naturalist, and as Bill recalls, she seemed a little ill at ease— plain looking, dressed in a long skirt, with high topped hiking shoes, outdoorsy brown colors, kind of a hippie style, no makeup or hair color and sporting lots of hand-crafted beads. Her address was in Kentfield, California. She was the picture of a Marin County tree hugger. She mentioned no ex-husbands, kids, boy or girl friends, only that she spent a lot of her time in one of Peru's remote jungle river ports on a small boat in the water of the Rio Tambopata in Puerto Maldonado, Peru.

She was creditable and seemed knowledgeable even though this seemed like it might be her "first rodeo," as a guide, and maybe we'd be her first clients as a result of the ad. Bill thought that she did seem to know what she was doing and felt very much at home in that part of the Amazon rainforest territory.

Fearis really outdid herself to accommodate Bill in planning a trip, insisting that it was exactly what we wanted. She might not be able to guide the trip herself because she was looking after her eighty-year-old mother with some health problems, but assured us that the guides, Victor and his crew—consisting of one small native named Jose—were very experienced and would take good care of us. They would know exactly the kind of tour to lead. "They don't speak any English but are very easy to communicate with," she assured Bill.

It sounded interesting to me too. I liked the idea of being able to be on our own with our own guides so that we could structure the trip to our interests and our pace. Bill also mentioned that we wanted to visit the lost city of Machu Picchu on the trip back to Lima. She had plenty of ideas for that too. Neither the visit to the old Inca capital of Cuzco nor Machu Picchu was possible on the trip I had researched and considered.

Bill and I met and hashed over what we had found, the pros and cons. We two subjective, half-brained planners were so enthusiastic about the "pros" that we could ignore the "cons." After brief discussion, we agreed on the Puerto Maldonado trip. It promised to be more of what we wanted—a look at the jungle itself. We hoped that our guides were the real thing.

Even though Bill and I had grown up in different environs, our bucket lists were very similar. Bill grew up in the suburbs of Chicago.

He was tall, with a Cro-Magnon/General McArthur looking face, very athletic. He could hit a golf ball a long way. He played the major sports; his father taught and coached. Because Bill had always lived in the suburbs, to him, an adventuresome traveling outdoor adventure was a fishing trip to Wisconsin. In his senior year he concentrated on baseball. He was a tall and lanky, long armed, fastball pitcher. He says he had a good curve also. I wasn't his catcher, but I have my doubts. He was good enough to obtain a baseball scholarship to University of Wyoming. It was there that he found his new world of mountains and prairie surroundings very intriguing. That sparked his great interest in other nontraditional, unexplored places and exciting experiences.

Eventually, high on his bucket list was exploring the Amazon rainforest jungle, diving on the Great Barrier Reef and visiting the African bush. From his early trips with his dad, he had a keen interest in all kinds of fishing.

Even though my parents were from the suburbs of Cincinnati, I grew up in the country, in rural Clermont County, several miles across the Little Miami River from Cincinnati. They liked the idea of living out in the country and having a barn where they could keep a few riding horses and some for their city friends. My dad never farmed; he worked in the city. During the Second World War years he worked at Wright Aeronautical in Cincinnati on the production line, building those powerful Wright Cyclone engines for the B-29 super bombers, usually on the night shift. Growing up on a farm, I had chores watching after someone's cattle, cleaning stalls, pitching hay, mending fences, watering and feeding horses and raising some chickens. Many times when I came home from school, hoping to go back to town and join a pick-up ball game, my mom would inform me that she had a call from Mr. Bickell down the road and one of the calves was stuck with his head under the fence or some gate was open and a couple cows were in someone's yard. The 360-

acre farm we rented was owned by an insurance man who kept 200 head of Herefords on the property, and part of our deal was to look after them. That would mean that I would have to get a scoop of oats and go out and coax my pony, Dynamite, to come over, then harness and saddle him and ride out to the problem. That sounded like an enviable cowboy-like life to some of the boys in the city, but it got to be just a time-consuming pain in the ass if you had to do it often and at all the wrong times.

Dad working on the night shift made the situation even more difficult for me. I had to do most of the daylight chores. For fun, I loved hiking in the woods shooting my single-shot 22 rifle at crows and squirrels, and collecting snakes for a hobby. My brother Denny was three years younger and Jack was born in 1946, while we were living in Mulberry. Whether our parents realized it or not, they raised their three sons as farm boys. We had some chickens, cattle, horses, dogs, and cornfields.

Traipsing through the woods was always special to me. I pictured myself in the African jungle or the Amazon someday. At a very early age, the Amazon was on my bucket list.

Sneaking out in the corn rows, stuffing some dried corn silk in a rolled-up page of a Captain Marvel comic book, lighting it and taking a few puffs was a big giggle. We were smoking. Ha. Like Bill, I played as many sports as I could at school. I went to tiny Mulberry grade school, where we had more than one grade in a room, and then to Milford, not far away. At that time, Milford High School seemed a bit of a risk academically, so we were sent into Cincinnati to the giant sized Withrow High School where our parents had gone.

From sports at Withrow, I had received a number of scholarship offers. I decided to take the football scholarship to Miami University in Oxford, Ohio. I remember talking to the head coach, Ara Parseghian, when I visited for a recruiting interview, and asking him if I could also go out for baseball if I came to Miami. I knew he would agree to it since he himself played football, and was a pitcher when he was a student there. I majored in geology and enjoyed all of the earth science courses I could take. Africa and the Amazon were still on my list for some time in the future.

During the last twenty years of my business career, I had traveled extensively in the world, but for both Bill and me, Amazonia seemed to be the "last frontier" on this planet. It was known to have completely different animals than those in Africa, Asia and North America: llamas, alpacas, jaguars, condors, capybara, huge snakes and fish we never see, including a lot of strange monkeys.

We could not even find field guides or any material on this vast and unique part of our globe, even though it was gigantic. One estimate I remembered was that probably 17,000 still unidentified, unstudied species of animals inhabited this area. If we had 400 known species of fish in North America, there were over 4000 in the Amazon, some of them even air-breathing. Some were similar to saltwater species but had adapted over the geologic ages from when the Amazon was a saltwater sea until the Andes pushed up and turned it into a forest draining fresh water from its vast mountain ranges. National Geographic mentioned that the rainforest might have millions of unidentified organisms including fish, insects and amphibians.

In the rainforest there were thought to be tribes of natives that had never seen people from the civilized world. They were reported to blow darts dipped in deadly poison from frogs, to shrink heads, and to brew hallucinatory concoctions from plants. There were hundreds of new trees in the rainforest, including the giant kapok and Brazil nut trees, and the rubber tree, which was the one thing that caused what little exploration and development there had been.

Chapter 3

Primed, Briefed, Conditioned and Keen

No one would ever have predicted the kind of enthusiasm and effort Fearis was putting into this project. She mostly wrote to us longhand, although some letters were typed. She drew diagrams and maps, sent clippings and suggested some animals and humans we might encounter in this expedition.

Fearis suddenly notified us that she would not be accompanying us because of her mother's ill health, which seemed to put her in a frenzy of assuring us that it would still be a great trip and we would be in good hands with her guides. She wrote page after page of advice: places to visit, alternatives, more possibilities, even Spanish notes we were to give people we might meet in Machu Picchu. She made lists of everything: foods, medicines, clothing, things to give the natives, hand-drawn maps, charts and recommendations on things we would never have considered, all in great detail. After one of her sixteen-page, hand-written almanacs, she must have had an afterthought and added a page 10A and 10B to put between pages 10 and 11.

Her writing was always upbeat; things seemed destined to be well organized, straightforward, time-tested, devoid of problems or inconvenience; no heavy lifting, no repairs, plenty of room, places for everything—good weather and great viewing, interesting food, a fascinating trip and adequate accommodations. All her suggestions were clear and complete. She could make a turd sound like a chorizo sausage, a deadly snake sound like a beautiful ribbon of color flowing effortlessly through the foliage with its own self-contained security system. This knack of hers would eventually cause us both endless entertainment and dismay—throughout the trip.

Every day was outlined. One example of one short day was typical:

"Day 2 – Early AM, fly to Puerto Maldonado. They stop in Cusco, sometimes you have to get off and sometimes you can wait on the airplane. If you get off, go directly to the waiting room and be attent. Make sure you are at the right gate. I think it is usually 1 or 2. There will be a lot of small, thick-chested Indian men. They are all gold washers that have been contracted to work the gold mines.

[followed by a sketch of the airport layout]

Arrive Puerto Maldonado. Spend the rest of day getting ready for jungle trip.

Day 2 continued. Lunch Califa – outdoor patio jungle food

See the local sights, dinner, giant catfish or picuru at the Danubio Azul. Main plaza. (Wow, a Blue Danube Restaurant in town?)

NO FIREARMS. Do not even think about it. You are only inviting trouble with a CAPITAL T. You would probably get thrown in jail as suspected terrorists, be mistreated, and have to pay huge bribes to get out after several weeks. Or you will be robbed, as the hotel people notice everything and who knows what could result. In the jungle, Victor and Jose ALWAYS carry a machete and know what to do in case of trouble.

(Hmm. Machetes vs. AK 47 machine guns? That was reassuring.)

"Restaurant Califa – lunch – (pitcher of chica morada)

Danubio Azul – dinner

Jungle Food: Pan de arroz - rice bread, Brazil nuts confectioned, fried fish – Pescado frito

Fish soup – chilcano

Stewed fish – piscado sudado

Roast deer – venado al horno

Best meat – picuro al horno

Fried yucca and bananas.

End Day 2"

Every day's description included what we might see, along with possible "picnic lunches" as she called the grub we would eat on the boat. Each day's description carried the same detail, or even more. She scrawled twenty-one pages of hand-written notes.

Copies were forwarded to me in Florida by Bill's wife, Sue, with her comment, "Here are some more. She writes, and writes, and writes and writes."

Included was a list of twenty or more food items we might want to bring: peanut butter, jelly and popcorn; even table salt because Peruvian salt is too coarse; gouda because it was in plastic; zip-lock bags containing seasoning, and tea; jerky, Mars Bars if we liked them; Tang; olives and a few other things. All of them had about as much chance of being in our bags as an unabridged Betty Crocker cookbook.

She recommended we bring baseball hats for the guides and some ballpoint pens and candy for the natives. Topping it off was a listing of no less than forty-eight separate items of provisions to be purchased locally by Victor, so that we could make certain he obtained them after we arrived.

Her medicine list included many things, like tonopan, coromina glucose, donofan, lomotil, and a can of condensed milk in case of vomiting. She wrote instructions for handling the effects of high altitude that sounded like we were preparing for a space mission. Although we both knew about the Pepto Bismol routine and started it before the trip, she included every imaginable item except a suicide kit of cyanide pills in case of capture. Had we taken seriously even a few of the list of health hazards and maladies for which she had prescribed preventions or cures, we should never even have considered this mission.

We did receive some clippings and other warnings of dangers in the area. There was an advisory from our U. S. State Department that cautioned that insurgency activity could pose increased dangers to visitors in Peru, including those in Lima, Cuzco and Machu Picchu. One guerrilla group, the Peruvian communist party's Shining Path, was marking its tenth anniversary and had stepped up attacks in sites frequented by tourists. Also, the U. S. Embassy received information that another guerrilla group, the Tupac Amaru Revolutionary Movement may be planning to kidnap foreigners, especially U. S. citizens. At our height of enthusiasm, Bill and I found it easy to ignore these things.

If we really wanted something more to worry about, we needed to look no further than the airline we were using. Eastern Airlines had been run for the past few years by the astronaut Frank Borman. In 1985, it was acquired by Frank Lorenzo, who was transferring a lot of its assets to his other airlines: Texas Air and Continental. Eastern also had survived labor problems and a crippling strike just the previous year. We could only hope our aircraft did not have a disgruntled pilot or a half tank of fuel.

In retrospect, it is difficult to imagine how we could have brushed these warnings aside. It must have been blind determination to go and the volume of other things we were trying to digest.

Fearis' best diagram was the organized, full page, top view of our riverboat, with drawings of each compartment and its use.

Beginning aft: the depiction of the engine and, going forward, two circular fuel tanks. -Gas.

The next section showed the compartment marked Food. A note explained - double waterproof tarp on the bottom and a covering over the top from sun.

Forward of that was a compartment marked: Cooking things, sleeping things, personal things. In front of that were "day packs" (a note said, "pile them so you can lean on them.")

The next section forward was marked: Sitting Platform – no shoes, with a side note "take shoes off – so you're not sitting in mud. Brush mud off railing and front of boat."

The bow section appeared to be quite large and was indicated as a place for Thermos & cups, Fishing equipment, shoes.

Maybe not clear, but it did look organized. The sitting platform was not configured, so where we would be parking buttocks for the entire ride would be a surprise.

* * *

As our flight from Miami headed west over the pitch-black Amazon basin, it cleared the last cordillera of the Andes in western Peru and made a large circle over the Pacific. The Andes reached as high as 20,000 feet in many areas we had crossed. No doubt the pilot had a lot of altitude to lose by circling before landing at sea level in Lima. Out the portside windows we could see the string of lights along the coast.

We finally touched down at the Lima airport, cleared immigration and customs and had a long wait for our bags to arrive. We were entertained by a dozen little natives involved in a noisy shoving contest to see who was going to help us. When the bags arrived, they looked bigger than the kids we selected from the flock to tote them.

The airport seemed like the best place to exchange our U. S. currency into Peruvian Intis. We could use dollars in charging hotel bills in Lima but in the smaller villages we would need local currency. In 1990, Peru was in the extreme of an inflation crisis and the Inti was becoming less valuable by the hour. In 1989, the inflation rate was 400% per year. This year it was also nearly 400%, so when I passed $200 across the counter at the exchange kiosk, the clerk handed me a huge wad of cash that came to about 800,000 Intis. Instantly rich. I only hoped that the rainforest town of Puerto Maldonado had not kept up with the international exchange rates, and we could be a pair of "super-rich gringos" from America.

We had been advised to take a black colored taxi, which we did. Naturally the Hotel Jose Antonio was on the other side of town, forty-five minutes from the airport. There may have been one farther, but we decided Fearis just hadn't known about it or she would have sent us.

As we neared the hotel we realized our driver was taking side streets. We came up to a roadblock with uniformed men, armed and waving us to stop. Our driver did some talking, so we passed by, moving around the barricade to the left. In about 100 yards, another barrier greeted us on the left side. I have never been comfortable with what appear to be kids waving guns like AK 47s and looking wide-eyed and frightened, as if they were expecting something to happen. These blockades were on alternating sides, all the way down the street, purposely preventing a vehicle to race straight toward the hotel.

Finally, at the hotel desk, I asked about what was going on, learning that there was an Andean Pact meeting and the president of Venezuela was having a cocktail reception party or something for the heads of state in this hotel, in honor of the newly elected president of Peru, Alberto Fujimori. I knew he was born in Peru—but a Japanese president? I couldn't help thinking how impossible it would have been in reverse: Imagine a Japanese-born Peruvian man named Ichiban Santiago elected Prime Minister of Japan.

* * *

Fujimori, son of an immigrant, studied in an agrarian school in Argentina, then at University of Wisconsin in Milwaukee and in Strasbourg, France. Now he was inheriting a country in dire economic straits with rampant inflation as well as the insurgency of organized communists. If that wasn't tough enough, after a few years, his wife publicly denounced him as corrupt and undemocratic (well what's new there?) and then she ran against him for president. He won that election separated from his wife, and named his daughter Keiko as "First Lady" of Argentina. Later he fled Peru and hid in Japan to escape charges of corruption, and formally resigned as president.

* * *

Well, they may have had the appearance of high security there in Lima that night, but it would have been very easy for Guillermo and me to have sashayed a black taxi down that street with a small dirty-bomb. Who would have known?

While we were registering at the front desk, I could feel uncomfortably close breathing behind me and the scent of really eye-watering, cheap perfume. I turned to look and was met by a big grin of white teeth surrounded by a heavy-duty load of red lipstick beneath a thick forest of false eyelashes. Friendly country, I guessed. At least she wasn't snapping her chewing gum in my ear.

Two bellboys grabbed our bags, took us to the elevator and punched in our numbers. The elevator stopped, opened and we expected to be in a hallway looking for numbers. Instead, we were in a large open room with a noisy party. A bar was set up there, attracting mostly well-dressed older men and a few heavily-lipsticked Señoritas like the heavy breather down in the lobby, smiling and serving drinks. Our view was blocked by two not-so-friendly-looking men asking us something. We held out our room keys and they motioned to get back on the elevator. We had accidentally stopped on the floor of the presidential cocktail party. Not feeling all that welcome, we returned to the elevator. Our bag boys checked our room numbers again and, this time, took us to the right floor.

Our room had only one king-sized bed. Oh, well, the two-man tent we were going to share for the next weeks was about half that size. Besides, I wouldn't have to tell anyone back home that I slept with Bill. About the time we dug out our Dopp kits and I found my Absolut bottle, the phone rang. A female voice chirped, "Buenos Noches, I see you een the lobby. You want party in you room? You come down - talk us."

I had visions of teeth and lipstick and could almost smell the perfume. She wasn't at the cocktails for Fujimori? She must have been a reject from the president's party. I guess it wasn't much trouble reading our room number, as close as she was, peering over my shoulder at the desk. We wondered what venereal disease table d'hote she might be offering this evening, but probably not polite to ask.

"Lo siento mucho, but we are not interested. Buenos Noches."

Bill and I laughed at the thought of these party rejects calling us as a last resort for some business at the hotel. Bill added, "How does that make you feel, Hammer? Pretty special, huh? Ha ha."

The phone rang again. I wasn't sure how long it would ring but we waited it out. We left an early wakeup call and hit the sack.

El Presidente Fujimori de Peru? Still sounds strange.

Above the river and its muddy banks, the impenetrable jungle with an exceptionally tall tree towering above the rest.

Chapter 4

Desolate Puerto Maldonado

After what felt like a short nap, we were up and on our way to the Lima airport in time to climb aboard Aero Peru flight 430 to Puerto Maldonado, with a stop at Cuzco. We still weren't ready to trust the tap water, so we had used a warm, fizzy mineral water from the little room supply to brush our teeth. I felt a little hungry, so I opened a couple of the small cans with the pictures of tomatoes on them. They tasted nothing like the picture; sort of reminded me of what I thought formaldehyde might taste like. Bill passed on the canned tomato juice, so I downed them both. Well, who knew when we would have a chance to eat again?

A closer look showed that they were canned Bloody Mary's, booze and all. Oops, I had two of them. Ugh.

The flight to Cuzco was in a vintage 727. I remembered that they were best used for flights where runways were short. This flight took us from sea level to an airport that was over 11,000 ft. in altitude. That's about twice as high as Denver. We landed with no cloud cover anywhere. It was clear and colors were vivid.

The stopover in Cuzco would last a couple of hours, so Bill and I decided to walk around town. The sky was especially clear and a dark shade of blue, the air crisp and dry. It felt like you could see forever. Distant mountain peaks were clear. Shadows were dark. Walking involved some climbing up steps and made us as winded as if we had finished a fifty-yard dash. We laughed at our heavy breathing after going uphill even a few steps to some shop. After panting our way around the town and trying to avoid the street people selling handmade necklaces and other trinkets, we boarded for the last leg of our flight to Puerto Maldonado. We looked forward to returning to Cuzco on the way home to take in the rich history of that city, seeing all the Inca stone works, artifacts and the natives.

In spite of the high altitude of Cuzco, flying southeast to the Amazon's rain forest valley meant climbing even higher over two more mountain ranges or cordilleras, which are twice the altitude of Cuzco, before dropping down to the valley. Even through our tired, droopy eyes we still had some magnificent new things to see. The snow-covered peaks in the distance seemed to rise with us as we gained altitude. Sharp, black ridges knifed through the snow where it was too steep to retain it. We needed our sunglasses.

After clearing the last mountain range, we gradually descended into this massive rainforest or jungle—what natives called the selva. From our high altitude and the perfectly clear sky, our visibility seemed to be more than a thousand miles. Our southeast heading gave us a panoramic view to the north and east. The jaw-dropping sight of this expansive green jungle stretching out to the horizon in every direction looked like a solid Kelly-green quilt, boundless and unbroken except for some long, thin, brown rivers that looped around like snakes in the lawn.

As we descended further, the irregularity of tree heights began to show and the forest looked more like a tight field of broccoli. For as far as we could see, the solid canopy seemed to cover the entire earth. There were no man-made breaks in the canopy anywhere, that we could see. No farms, houses, cleared areas or different terrain. There was no trace of man or animal.

Trees were mostly all the same height, but occasionally very tall ones soared above the canopy. Now and then a tall one with a reddish tint stood out.

How did nature space these giants among them and what were they? The jungle canopy was a perfect cover for the ground beneath, too thick to see anything. Every tree was competing for its share of sunlight and there was no space left open. Bill envisioned big fish hidden everywhere below, while I imagined jaguars and boa constrictors.

We were a very long way from home.

As massive as this vista seemed, I knew we were looking at only a tiny part of Amazonia's three million square miles, a sprawl as large as the entire United States, covering most of seven countries in South America. And it is all trees and water, no mountains, canyons, plains or desert.

We continued on and on with no break in the scenery. After a while I turned away to look at the map for a couple of minutes and Bill jabbed me. "Hey look at this, we're going down in this damn jungle."

We were landing. The runway wasn't visible, only the cut trees in a solid wall to the left. It seemed to be on a downhill slope. Just before touching down, the only ground we could see was rust-colored dirt and the trees on either side, which looked like long, bare poles with leafy tops. Obviously, this runway was cut right out of the jungle.

The reverse thrust of the engines to bring us to a stop seemed to be in an emergency mode, full-power braking, as if we were running out of runway. When we slowed to taxi speed and turned, we still could not see much of an airport. It was a runway and a small building in a jungle opening. Near the end of the runway there stood a line of open, thatched-roof structures. The pilot told us, "Bienvenidos a Puerto Maldonado..." so we knew we were at the destination, anyway.

Puerto Maldonado.

We saw some native Indios near the shelters, an old pickup truck, motor scooters, banana trees and some chickens. Over by a cluster of trees we spotted a pair of red bi-planes and a few more chickens. Could the Red Baron have escaped Germany and settled here in the jungle?

"We're here," Bill said. "We are supposed to look for the guys with the baseball hats." I still wasn't sure whether we made an emergency landing in a jungle opening or had been hijacked to some gang hideaway. This was a very tiny place, the first of many of Fearis' embellishments.

Soon I noted one of the short men with a baseball hat. It turned out to be Jose Burga, the boat's crewman, standing near a pickup truck that had overhead rails in the bed and a heavy coating of local dust. It was the only large vehicle in the row of waiting people on foot or with scooters. Jose was a nice-looking man, not with the normal wide face and nose of most of the natives, but sharper features. Actually handsome until he broke into a big grin and displayed a few missing teeth. He seemed to keep a thoughtful, intelligent demeanor most of the time. I guess we would all kill for that smooth tan skin. (Speaking for myself and my sunburning Celtic friends.) He made himself known to us and repeated his name, "Jose, Jose."

We exchanged names and shook his small, hard, calloused hand. Since Jose had started waving at us the minute we stepped out of the plane, I guess we were a pair of conspicuous gringo turistas. Contrary to Fearis' earlier declaration, "They don't speak English but they are easy to communicate with," it seemed to us that Jose had never even heard a word of English. Even his Spanish was a bit different.

When the bags arrived, Jose hired a barefoot guy to fight for ours. They were tossed in the bed of the truck and Guillermo and I were invited to jump in after them, along with a few other travelers, and we were off to our high-end hotel.

We must have made quite a spectacle: a bunch of men standing up in the back of a pickup, hanging on to a pipe structure with a plume of red dust in our wake. Judging by the number of other riders in this truck bed, this must have been public transportation. A few jumped off at different stops. We were the last to be delivered to our destination, giving us a chance to sight-see in our new 'hood.

Puerto Maldonado is an unlovely pioneer town with wooden stores on both sides of the unpaved dirt streets. No roads or railroads to any other town or anywhere else existed. Only a single runway airport and the rivers provided any access to this place; there are no cities anywhere nearby.

One other little omission by our "naturalist" travel advisor soon became obvious: no electricity in this city either. Those would seem to be a couple of major detractors from a place that she wanted to call our "home base" city.

The only thing missing in this pioneer town were hitching posts and a saloon with swing doors.

During the rubber boom in the Amazon valley in the late 19th century, the city of Manaus, in central Brazil, grew to be the primary business headquarters location, near the junction of three of the sprawling river systems that drain much of this giant rainforest known as Amazonia. From there, year by year, harvesters of latex began working farther and farther upstream, thousands of streams. This area is the farthest and most remote, no matter which route you took. Exploring this area for the Peruvian government in 1901, Don Juan Villalta established this location at the confluence of the Madre de Dios and the Tombopata, naming it for Faustino Maldonado, an earlier explorer who had drowned in a nearby rapids. Maybe Maldonado was not the most heralded of names, but since the rubber boom was about to bust, maybe it was appropriate to name it after a man who drowned here.

Little did we know that this dusty Ford pickup was the first class limo in town and the only four-wheeled vehicle we would ever see here.

We had a lot to learn about proper riding in the back of a pickup truck on bumpy unpaved roads, especially following a cloud of dust from any vehicles ahead of us. We learned a lot of it on this first half-hour long ride to the hotel, lessons we can share.

Guillermo & Lee's Peruvian Pickup Truck Protocol:

-Sightseeing from the back of a truck is impossible unless you want dust in your eyes or you wear goggles.

-Don't sit down on anything; your derriere will bruise, or you might ruin a kidney, bite your tongue or chip some teeth.

-Hold onto the overhead rails at all times or you will be thrown out onto the "unpaved" road. Using both hands is recommended.

-Squint and look backward—if you must look.

-Don't straighten your legs. Keep them flexed like sea legs so you can absorb the bumps.

-Use only hats that are tied down and be ready to duck limbs.

-Don't wear or take anything you don't want dusty, wet or decorated with avian droppings.

-Don't try to eat or chew tobacco or you will break one or more of the above rules.

The only vehicular transit in Puerto Maldonado.

At last we arrived. So, this was the real "Day 2" of our Fearis travel plan? We unloaded our duffel bags at the Hotel de Turistas, its name prominently displayed over its porch with three stars under it. We hauled everything up the wooden steps and into the small office. Bellboys are non-existent in the bush country. A fat, droopy-eyed desk clerk didn't bother standing up, just put a paper out for us to sign and pushed two old room keys our way. He looked like someone who had just been annoyed by having been wakened from his hangover nap and barely aware of where he was and about as excited to see us as he would be to see a pint of cold urine. I was already homesick for the over-the-shoulder, cheap-perfume smell of the night before.

We were given separate rooms on the first—and only—floor, about four rooms apart. The hallways smelled musty or moldy, like an old attic. The room smelled older and the beds resembled something you see out front of a shack on garbage collection day in the wrong neighborhood. The only window in the room was too high to see out—no room with a view. But, by the looks of the town as we rode through it, this might be a positive amenity. It was permanently open but, luckily, screened.

On one side of the room an almost white, rusting, sheet metal shower enclosure, with no curtain or closure, abutted an old toilet with a blackish, rust-stained bowl. Neither of these appliances was operable except from 6:00 to 7:30 PM, when the hotel generator was turned on. We had no trouble knowing when it was running; it sounded like a jack hammer in the room next door. An eating area with three booths near the office was open "when necessary," between the same 6:00 to 7:30 "generator time." Even a phone call was a possibility if made by the office in advance during that same magic "generator time" if the one and only telephone was not tied up by some outsider on the town's party line. As might be expected, we could find no radio, TV, phone or light. Except for a few small vehicles, and the "generator time," we might as well be living in a run-down Mexican border town in the 1880s.

After check-in, Jose took us out in the town to a restaurant, riding tripled on the back of his Honda scooter. We were surprised his tires didn't blow out with all that weight. The restaurant occupied a shed behind a shack. There were three tables with plastic tablecloths, chickens in the backyard, dogs, a cat and a banana tree. There we met our guide and captain, Victor Yarikawa. He was a sun-darkened Japanese Peruvian, like an offspring of Pocahontas and Hirohito. He wore a serious, if not slightly frowning, worried expression at all times. Having done so much business in Japan, I almost bowed and greeted him with a "konbawa" but realized he was a couple of generations away from Japan and spoke only Spanish or a local language.

We ate a big fish they called "dorado," washed it down with some weird yellow stuff, and ate fried bananas. The name dorado, where we come from, is Spanish for an ocean fish we call "dolphin fish" (the key being the word "fish.") Now, restaurants mostly call it by its Hawaiian name, "mahi mahi," so that people don't think we are eating Walt Disney's trained dolphin mammal, Flipper. The names of fish around the world are puzzling, probably because they were all named locally before some world dictionary could sort out the differences. This dorado, in this place in Puerto Maldonado, in fact, was a catfish.

Victor was interesting, friendly. He ordered for us and tried to explain all the local food the restaurant served. He seemed especially pleased to point out that the things we were stuffing in our faces were local and from this part of Peru – "aqui, aqui." Well, that was no big deal. Unless it came in by plane, on that flight we were on, it had to be local.

Some of Victor's and Jose's friends or acquaintances would wander through the room, filled with curiosity about this strange pair of aliens from outer space. They were looking us over and chatting with Victor, who would then mention our trip down the rio and in the selva (jungle). One of them started jabbering in an alarming tone, warning us, "...cuidado con los murcielagos rabiosos." We found out later that he was talking about how sixty people had died recently after being attacked and bitten by rabid bats in the jungle. Sixty people!

That would take a little luster off one's pursuit of native wildlife.

Damn, we didn't fly over the Andes to engage rabid bats. Sixty people? That's more than serious. Guillermo and I both decided that any cave explorations that might be in Victor's plans were now scratched.

After this lunch it was time to discuss what provisions they should acquire and give them the money to buy them. They asked for so little money that it wouldn't make any difference if they even had a little profit figured in.

The language problem was as amusing as it was frustrating. We mostly got the job done. Jose held up a gallon bottle of water. I immediately said, "Si, compra muchas. Doce botellos, OK? Doce," I repeated, showing ten fingers, then two. I remembered Fearis' diagram of the boat and knew there was ample room in the bow of our vessel for a dozen gallon jugs of freshwater bottles. That should do us for coffee and drinking—maybe. I assumed, of course, that he was referring to clean, bottled water. We probably should not drink from the tap, so we surely couldn't drink from the river.

Bill and I had very little more to say. We left the food supplies mainly to them. We hadn't been inspired to bring the Fearis Frenzy inventory list for them to purchase; instead, we mainly packed a few things of our own like Pepto Bismol, Lomotil, Tums, a "just-in-case antibiotic," a few granola bars, peanut butter and other over-the-counter stuff. Bill was much more concerned that he had his giant Rambo-style knife with him. It was his ever-ready companion—a combination machete, survival knife, saw and sharp carving blade in a military holster.

I felt the same about my 35MM Canon camera. Ever-ready.

We gave Victor the amount of money he said he needed to buy provisions, which was about $150 worth of Intis or about 560,000 Intis. He seemed more than satisfied and jammed it quickly into his pocket.

As the big spender I was, I picked up the dinner tab of 14,375 Peruvian Intis or about $3.75 for all four of us, and worth every cent. I threw in a 2,000 Inti tip, for which I received a big smile and a "Gracias, gracias, gracias."

I have a feeling that during this fast run-up in inflation and the high-speed, hourly fluctuations of their exchange rates, this tiny jungle town was more than a little late in receiving this kind of news and were uninvolved in the international currency fluctuations and, therefore, happily immune.

We were dropped back at the hotel after lunch with plans to meet Jose at the hotel in the morning and haul our gear down to the boat. During the generator running time, I turned on the shower. At least I thought I did. It drooled only a little stream of cold, rusty water. A shower was out of the question.

I suddenly remembered back before the trip, when I had read that scant page and a half on this town of Puerto Maldonado, in the book, "Peru, a Travel Survival Kit," that this Hotel de Turistas was the only place mentioned under Places to Stay – high end. Charges $7.50/12.50 per day. The three others were listed under low end. Charges $1.30/2.00 per day. What were they like—dungeon cells with rats and a bed of nails? Cat-o-nine tails for wake-up calls? Those prices had been printed years earlier, of course, and with the major Inti meltdown, they were even lower in dollars.

Bill suggested we go down to the small eating area at generator time and see what's what, maybe a bite for dinner. We were sitting at a table when an English-speaking guest came in. He seemed surprised to see us and struck up a conversation. He stood about six feet tall, wore a short beard, khaki clothes and appeared to be in his 60s. He was as curious about what we were doing here as we were about him.

He reminded me of several people I had met here and there in some strange places in the world that I considered "Internationals." Typically, he was born in the U. S., moved to Australia as a kid, lived in England and other places, always working in some foreign business. In his case, it was mining for large and small companies. Then he moved back to Australia or Spain. (Or any other combination of places.) They are comfortable anywhere, know the travel tricks, a couple of languages, have little or no serious current family affairs but lots of strange histories, and low comfort levels. These adventuresome people seemed unattached and always waiting to stumble over El Dorado, the legendary hidden culture with gold everywhere.

This man, we soon learned, had come to own parts of three working placer gold mines in the Madre de Dios area, operating in several parts of the river.

Placer mines scoop up gravel and sand from running streams and separate out gold dust and small nuggets by running the sand-laden water at just the right speed over a material that catches the heavier gold fragments while letting the other material flow back to the stream. You might call it conveyor line panning for gold. Mandatory, of course, in any operation handling physical gold, is having a trusted partner-overseer of the operation, one who is happy with his share and other considerations, plus workers on the line, without pockets. It is also important to have one of the workers as a secret partner, watching the others.

Living permanently in Australia, he visited his various interests periodically. His name was Stan something; neither of us could remember his last name because of a strange repeating quirk in his conversation that made us call him by a nickname all the time. He liked to talk. Whenever he came to a pause at the end of thought, he would say, "Well... any who." To us, he became instantly and forever, Mr. Any-who.

The best attribute of Mr. Any-who was that he had bought some ground beef, or ground something, and had made a meatloaf. He was willing to share it and we found it a great last supper before hitting the muddy flow. Any-who told us again about the sixty some people who had died from rabid bat bites. He was curious about our trip and what we were doing. He thought it was interesting but a little crazy—a perfect description of our adventure. He said he was going to be around for a while so he hoped to see us again. We did too.

Bill and I went to our rooms at dark. We needed some sleep and I had set my travel alarm for sunrise. Our plan was that Jose would meet us in the morning and we would haul our stuff down the road to the marina nearby, where we would find Captain Victor waiting with the boat.

The air was stale and heavy. Perspiration dampened every bit of clothing. I stumbled into that uncomfortable, sagging bed with my head full of negative thoughts. I could hear some dogs barking, bugs slamming into the screened window and a tapping sound as if I was in a room full of old-fashioned typewriters clacking away. It was strange. I couldn't stop wondering what that tapping was and how I was going to sleep with that endless clattering.

I entertained a few thoughts about how far we were from civilization, hospitals, electricity, any kind of emergency help, or people with whom we could talk, the conditions of this dump we were in, and the tents we were going to use for shelter when once in the jungle.

Having traveled on business and vacation for the last twenty years, mostly internationally, I had given little thought to the fact that there were many areas of the undeveloped world with which I was not familiar. It had never occurred to me that there were cities anywhere that one could access via commercial airline that had no other forms of access. There were no roads connecting this town to any other part of Peru. One could not go to or from Puerto Maldonado and Lima by car, train or boat. In fact, there was no commercial water transportation and no towns anywhere within any reasonable distance with transportation, either.

It was about then when I heard the unmistakable gnawing of rats in the ceiling.

Who in hell was conducting this concert?

The rats had started all at once, as if cued, and the grinding noise was continuous. The night was already hot and sticky, now noisy? The rats' gnawing got louder, and I felt a strange "trapped" feeling. I began to sweat. What were we getting into? This was supposed to be our comfortable base camp. From here we go out and rough it? If all goes well, we get back to this paradise in a fortnight?

In that moment, the excitement of this trip was being overshadowed by the discomforts. I was getting anxious and a little angry—at myself.

I took a shoe and threw it up against the ceiling as hard as I could. The rats' grinding stopped. I did not hear them scurry away, however. I folded over the near empty pillow, put my head down and continued to wonder about the tapping sound. I got out of bed but I could not see out the high window. Finally, I remembered that large trees grew nearby and shed very large leaves. Stiff, dried leaves covered the ground. Moisture was probably condensing as the night cooled. It dripped off the trees and the roof onto these big, dry leaves, making a tapping sound. That was it. There was no stopping it. A shoe wouldn't help that.

After the rats had been silent for at least thirty seconds, they started up again, gnawing with even greater vigor, like trying to make up for the down time caused by my thumping shoe interruption. They had taken up residence right over my head. What if their gnawing chewed through and rats fell on me? It flashed through my mind that the possibility of falling rats was the very inspiration for the development of the canopy over four-poster beds. This bed had none. Why were they gnawing anyway if it wasn't to cut through the ceiling?

Oh hell, what fun.

The rat crunching and the leaf clacking probably wouldn't have bothered me if it hadn't been for a sudden claustrophobic feeling that came over me. It was a feeling of anxiety about what we were about to do, with no easy way out. I was sweating more profusely. This was a very uncomfortable place, with no relief—and we were committed to go even deeper into this jungle.

Strangely, I knew what an anxiety attack was.

Although I have never been prone to anxiety problems or depression, I did have an experience one time. It occurred a few years earlier, when I was planning to get married. I had a long day of feeling as if I was going to be put in a strait jacket, stuffed into a box and abandoned in a dark cellar. I couldn't even see colors that day. The world had turned gray.

The next evening, I called the whole thing off. A few days later, it took only a visit to a skilled counselor and just minutes for her to ask me some penetrating questions. As I listened to my own answers, I knew this was a simple problem, a routine thing to her, and she began to smile and laugh. That laugh told me all I really needed to know.

She smiled as she said, "You're just having a little anxiety attack. You shoulda seen Raymond in the office across the hall. Ha, he was a basket case. I know that you two have no real problems. You won't even need to come back."

She was right. When I knew what had just happened, the anxiety was gone. I never had a single bit of remorse or any second thoughts after that.

In this case, however, I was ready to cancel the rest of this trip. We were deep in the middle of a far-off jungle—hot, hungry, and thirsty, without a convenient escape. We were in the hands of two little local hombres about whom we had serious doubts. To start with, they couldn't speak English. Even their Spanish was strange. We were preparing to go even deeper tomorrow and for many more days. This wasn't an Abercrombie and Kent luxury tour. We were on our own, alone, except for this pair of

Peruvian rednecks, one of whom was native Indian. The other was probably a third-generation samurai or something, born and raised in this jungle frontier.

My bottle of Absolut vodka was also empty, gone for the duration.

I finally thought this was serious enough to warrant some discussion. I was perspiring heavily now and decided to go down the hall and wake up Bill, so I did. He had been happily asleep. I easily saw that he had no problems and was completely ready to enjoy this trip, not really bothered by the noises. His rats must have been quieter.

I shut up, sucked it up and decided I would enjoy the trip. Discussion over.

I went back to my broken mattress under the rat serenade, next to that outdoor typing pool, launched one more shoe at the ceiling, enjoyed a short silence, and tried to sleep. Tomorrow we were going to chug down the muddy Tombopata to the Rio Madre de Dios with El Capitan Victor Yarikawa de Puerto Maldonado and crew.

Captain Yarikawa—still sounded strange.

Chapter 5

Down the Mighty River

W e didn't need an alarm the next morning. The chickens started their crowing competition just before dawn. I got up and dressed for the jungle cruise. I could hear Guillermo down the hall cramming things into the duffel and grunting as he pulled on his new mesh combat boots he'd bought at the army surplus. He thought they would be perfect for this trip. We met in the hall and lugged our duffels and canteens out the front door. We munched a couple of granola bars while the half-dressed, drowsy Mr. Excitement, the desk clerk, yawned and with his eyes still at half-mast, checked us out. I coughed up a few Intis for him and brightened his day by telling him we would return in a couple weeks, to which he responded with a yawn and a head turn. He was certainly a gracious and helpful host and valuable asset for this Inn and its 0.3-star rating.

The boat crew, Jose, met us at the door with a young helper. A bunch of little street urchins followed us. It seemed that their mothers could always find a T-shirt to put on them but not pants or shoes. It must have been a sign of courage for them to get close to us. They would innocently and carefully edge over near us and put a hand on our duffels. Actually touching our gear was the ultimate coup for them. When they had finally made their touch, they would giggle and go back to join the others.

A native canoe - only way to travel in this area is by river.

We schlepped our packs and provisions down the dirt roadway past shacks full of residents who had crowded together to see this spectacle: Two loco Americano hombres dragging all this gear down the road to a mud bank, seventy feet above their big muddy river.

"There it is, Hammer. Take a look at that big brown thing," Guillermo said as we had our first overlook at the Tombopata River. It was about 300 yards wide at this point. I stopped to take a picture. A lone dugout canoe with an Indio paddler and his squaw worked slowly upstream. With no wind, the water was almost glassy smooth and the river so wide that it was almost impossible to see that there was current moving at about three miles per hour. The dirt pathway from the road led directly down to the water, beside a small thatched shelter with two canoes pulled up together near the bank of the river.With a closer look, we could see Victor standing in the smaller of the two boats. Guillermo said something that sounded like "Ho-lee sheeeut, that can't be our boat!"

I agreed that it was too small, so I reassured him, "No, that's probably the launch (a canoe) that he will use to take us to the boat we will take on the cruise. It's probably over at the marina they mentioned."

Victor and Jose were packing things in the boat with the little helper handing them in from the bank. As I approached the bank, I handed Capitan Victor my camera bag and asked, "Where is the marina, Victor? Donde esta?"

"Si, marina, si marina. Aqui. No problema."

No problem? Also, not the answer I was looking for. Another cold splash of reality hit me and was now soaking in. This WAS the marina and this thing WAS our cruise ship.

Bill and I spent a minute staring at each other, stunned. Neither of us could believe it. This damn thing was only about 25 feet long, pointed on both ends, and about four feet of beam at the widest part.

At one end was mounted a small 16-horsepower Briggs and Stratton gasoline motor with an eight-foot drive shaft sticking out the stern driving a small propeller. The boat was made of bare hardwood, well weathered. The propeller itself was encased in a small metal rib cage so that the spinning blades themselves wouldn't contact the bottom or other objects. Attached to the motor mount was the tiller, handled by the crew, Jose. There was only a forward gear or neutral. For reverse, Jose would have to swing the shaft around to the side so that it propelled us backward, at a rather obtuse angle. It was an awkward move for Jose to make. To coast, he would push down on the tiller, raising the blades out of the water, then disengage the prop or shut off the motor.

The original keel, like all their local riverboats, was a hollowed hardwood log with sides built up with shiplap planking. Four people plus all that gear and provisions seemed too heavy to me, but it floated—uncomfortably low in the water. Two drums of fuel hunkered in the rear.

In addition to our duffels, I counted two tents, pots and pans, groceries—and then I remembered, "Oh yeah, Jose, did you get the agua? Twelve bottles? Doce botellos de agua, Jose?"

To that, Jose held up a slightly mud smudged, plastic gallon jug of water. Yes, he clearly understood. I acknowledged with a smile and said, "Si, Jose. Cuantos mas?" hoping to see the other eleven jugs in the bow.

He held up only the one jug, thrusting it at me again with his half grin, saying, "Si, agua."

Huh? Was that it? One jug only? "Solo uno?"

He said he couldn't find any more or something like that, in his high-speed chatter mode, but not to worry because he would boil the river water. I had to look up the words "Hervimos el agua," or something like that. I was too shocked to believe he meant it. He said he would show us later.

Bill and I looked at each other in disbelief. Did he just tell us we were going to have to drink water from this river of mud, piranha poop, Indio sewage and who knows what other poisons? The whole trip?

Pepto Bismol, do your stuff.

I was steaming. I'm sure my face turned the color of frustration, anger and helplessness, whatever hue that is, but I managed a fake smile and said, "Guillermo, this lilsumbitch is trying to kill us."

Bill looked at me and smiled, "What makes you think that he didn't just fill that jug from his kitchen tap water to make us happy?"

Jose kind of smiled as if he had been congratulated. I was now seriously worried about what we were going to do for water on this trip. That was about when we began to call the two of them by some politically incorrect terms like those original expletives you could hear from the depths of the smoke filled "cave" at Thorngate at the same exact moment someone slammed down what was left of a losing gin rummy hand.

From that time on, Bill and I did entertain ourselves by slurring a variety of endearing pejoratives at our guides while smiling, just to check whether they understood any of them. We called them things that might even make the cave dwellers back home blush. A man can derive a great deal of stealthy, personal amusement looking another man in the face, smiling and calling him something that would normally get you punched or shot and having the man smile and nod his head in agreement and appreciation. Smiling and looking at Jose and say, "You little prick, you are a stupid-looking asshole." They didn't recognize the sounds—just the smiles—and they would give us a grateful smile back. It was our private amusement. The higher the x-rating, the more fun.

Who knows, they may have been doing the same thing between each other.

Bill and I were directed to a plank across the boat in the center. We were to sit there, side by side, facing forward. Behind us were our duffel bags. This heavily laden boat floated crouched in the muddy water, with only about five inches of freeboard. Bill and I could touch the water with our hands just gripping the gunwale while sitting there. A small wave from the side or a slight list, and we were going to get wet.

As we sat there with our rears nearly at water level, the water at our sides, we couldn't help thinking about Fearis' description of our organized cruising vessel. This must have been the "sitting platform"—a real observation area.

We asked the crew, Jose, to take a farewell photo of us from the shore. After instructions on where to look and which button to push, he snapped a few, had some bystander take one with him in it, then handed back the camera and boarded. Bill said, "What about the hats? Should we give them now?" It was the right time. We reached in our duffels and pulled out the two hats we were going to present to them. We gave Jose a white cap from the Oldsmobile Scramble golf tournament (a national golf tournament back when there were Oldsmobiles) and gave Victor a dark blue cap that said "Captain" in gold letters, the bill covered with scrambled egg embellishments that are the sign of very high rank in every military uniform in the world.

They were ecstatic. I think they slept in them the rest of the trip and maybe for the rest of their lives.

Jose started the little two-cycle engine. It sputtered and coughed and didn't sound much like something our lives might depend upon. The natives usually use dugouts and paddles, and the jungle is quiet, so the loud sound of the motor made the little barefooted, bare-bottomed kids that followed our every move, call them "pecke peckes."

Victor pushed off the bow with his long paddle, while Jose steered us out into the current, which swung the bow to point downstream. We were off. Four guys, two pairs of strangers, without a common language, in a loaded pecke-pecke, headed toward the expansive confluence of the Tambopata and the Madre de Dios rivers somewhere in the Amazon rainforest.

Bill and I swallowed hard and braced ourselves for a look at this whole new world that we always wanted and planned to see. It would be an eye opener.

After rounding our first big bend in the river, a glance backward told me that we could no longer see Puerto Maldonado—or any other vestige of human life.

Bill inserted a small wad of Redman's chew in his cheek as we moved out. We floated on this shiny mud surface surrounded by a forest of many different species of trees, all fighting for sunlight. One got the impression that if there was so much as a small opening of light coming through the canopy, some tree would shoot up a twig toward it and throw up a leaf to cover it. The forest floor was almost dark.

Even though I had shed last night's anxiety over our isolation here, every turn of the river gave me a little nudge that we were going deeper and deeper into this labyrinth. I shooed away the thought as much as possible, and Bill and I continued to enjoy all this new world of things we had never seen in our lives. We certainly could not think more about returning today or tomorrow. I put it off for now. The camera was more important. I wanted it to stay dry and ready.

Bill kept the vigil for any sight of animal life. Where was it?

Chapter 6

Downstream and Farther

The water in the thousands of rivers that drain this Amazon valley are considered to be of three types: clear, black or white. Clear rivers are those that drain over rocky areas of land. Black are the ones with a lot of decomposed plant material. White are the rivers with a lot of so-called "nutrients." The word "nutrients" must include mud because this so-called white river was definitely brown. It could only be considered white like a cup of coffee with cream in it could be considered "white." It was as much mud as water. Objects could be seen only within inches of the surface.

We wondered what we were missing below the muddy flow. It struck us both how really great it would have been if it was as clear as the lakes and streams in Ontario and we could witness the strange menagerie of fish and other creatures below.

There seemed to be some familiar looking birds like herons and ibises, but a complete absence of swimming birds: no ducks, terns, sea gulls or pelicans. Maybe they didn't want muddy butts or flesh-eating fish nipping at them. Of course, pelicans couldn't see the fish in this water so diving on them would be out.

This morning it was a smooth flowing lake as we moved out into the merger with the Madre de Dios River, which seemed to be an even darker brown. Like any body of water, while still, it took on the reflections of the sky, the shoreline of trees or sunlight. The blending of the rivers was hardly noticeable. The water just became wider and El Capitan Victor moved us farther from the banks. The endless river bends kept us from looking very far ahead, adding more mystery to this strange venture.

The appearance of the jungle varied greatly depending on its elevation from the river. Any trees on the bank or on the forest floor were bare and muddy up to the rainy season's high-water level. These trees were under water at least part of the year and had no limbs below the high-water mark. The trunks were smooth, sheathed in a thin coat of mud. The forest floor was bare or with matted grasses, no heavy underbrush.

The giant Brazil nut and kapok trees grew on higher ground where the forest was heavier with bushes and vines. After a few miles, Jose handed forward two bags of Brazil nuts from the stash near him. The bags were not pretty but the nuts were delicious. One bag revealed nuts covered with powdered sugar; the others offered plain ones. We tortured ourselves with thoughts of washing down these nuts with a tall, cool drink. But then, I guess old Francisco Pizzaro didn't have iced drinks either, and he was here for very long trips and didn't die of dehydration.

I turned around to Jose at the tiller and asked him if he had any change from the money I had given him for provisions. "Tiene cambio, Jose?" giving him the universal sign for cash, rubbing the thumb and index finger. That got me only an understanding nod, no Intis. I had my hand outstretched but he only smiled.

"Si, cambio, si, cambio."

But he never gave me any. Maybe he was waiting until cocktail hour.

It was hard to imagine water ten to twelve feet higher than this river during their rainy season. The river must have flooded through miles of forest and been many times wider. It deposited many layers of mud during flood season, varying in color from oyster to tortilla, to slate, and shades of rust. These different colors of mud were now eroding as the river lowered. The riverbanks we passed displayed these layers like small road cuts or canyon walls. The Spanish word for mud is lodo and there were loads of lodo layered everywhere, in all colors.

Our captain seemed to hug the banks more than steaming down the center of the river. It was getting hotter and stickier. The only sounds were created by the little motor on our boat. White herons flew over, and then some monkey screeched and the shrill pihas bird whistled loudly, sending shivers up our backs. We knew for sure that we were now in the jungle. No houses, roads, fences, crops or any trace of humanity. No airplane contrails were anywhere to be seen in the clear blue sky.

One experiences a special feeling of exhilaration and awe in seeing natural, untouched land. No electricity, TV, telephone or radio available. Eventually there came the eerie realization that this is actually a prehistoric look at a part of the world. Nature without human touches anywhere. Changes will surely happen: settlement, clearing, lumber, harvesting, power and infrastructure. But now, this is what the first explorers saw. Only the results of the natural, annual flooding of this river made any mark in this magnificent dense forest.

I kept my Canon 35mm loaded with color slide film. It was close by, in the duffel, where I could grab it. There was no end to the things I wanted to record. I just hoped I had enough film.

Photos from a moving pecke-pecke have the double problem of a moving, tossing boat and the vibration of the little engine.

Unlike digital photos of today, we would have to wait until we returned to see what was captured on film.

It seemed that we were going downstream at a fast pace. We estimated twelve to fifteen miles per hour. The motor propelled us at idle speed to keep us navigable and straight while the current was moving at various speeds, depending on the width of the stream at the time. As it narrowed, we picked up speed. The Bernoulli principle was in demonstration right in front of us, but of little use to us. Hell, we could hardly calculate even where we would get our next drink of water.

* * *

The Rio Madre de Dios has its source in the Andes. There are two mountain ranges, or cordilleras, between the ancient Inca city of Cuzco and the lower jungle town of Puerto Maldonado. The first is the Cordillera Vilcanota and, east of that, the Cordillera Carabaya. By air, the distance from Cuzco to Maldonado is about 200 miles, but it is many times farther when actually travelling on the looping, meandering rivers.

The source of the Madre de Dios is in Vilcanota, cascading, and twisting down 10,000 feet to the rainforest valley below, heading toward the northeast, there met by the Manu River after its similar journey from the mountains northwest of it. The river then starts its flow eastward. Like a giant brown snake winding through the jungle another sixty miles or so, it is joined and fed by the Inambari River from the right. This enlarged Madre de Dios then begins to wind through the jungle on its eastward path but takes a sharp turn north for ten miles, meets another river, and twists its way back to where it started, nearly doubling back on itself.

As it reaches the point near its original turn, it converges with the large Tombopata River, which has descended from the high mountains of the Cordillera Carabaya. It was at that very confluence that the jungle was cleared and this little village,

Puerto Maldonado, was settled in the early 1900s, in expectation of the expanding rubber business that never happened.

This broader Madre de Dios then travels an irregular path eastward into Northern Bolivia for hundreds of miles, eventually into Brazil, joining the massive Madeira River system. The Madeira is a major tributary of the Amazon that collects much of the water from Southern Brazil, Northern Bolivia and Eastern Peru. It merges with the Amazon River at a point east of the city of Manaus.

From there the Amazon is a massive body of water. At its mouth at the Atlantic Ocean it becomes the largest discharge of freshwater into the ocean anywhere on Earth. Probably the largest outflow of lodo, too. It is often reported that ships as far out in the Atlantic Ocean as 100 miles from the mouth of the Amazon can dip freshwater from the sea.

* * *

After we had traveled a couple of hours downstream, the river seemed to split into two equal channels, each going off into its own path through the jungle. I was puzzled. I had studied streams, rivers, the different stages of erosion and ages of rivers as part of my major in geology. I could recognize features and shapes that existed in young, old and mature streams. It was not natural for rivers to branch off downstream into new rivers. They are all part of a drainage pattern that has them merging until they reach the mouth. Then, maybe there are some bayous splitting at its delta. We were thousands of miles from anything like that.

It turned out that a mile or two farther down this new stream, we were rejoined by that wandering branch that seemed to have left us. We had actually been going around a large island that split the river. This happened many more times on this trip. No doubt that these big river islands were remnants of the total riverbed during the flooded rainy season. They had trees on them, small ponds, lots of lodo and were favorite places for herons, spoonbills and other big wading birds.

After what seemed like hours, we made our first docking on the mud bank. It was sort of a pit stop to get out, take care of business and maybe explore the jungle for the first time. It was then and there that we learned our first difficult lessons in disembarkation on the muddy bank of a fast-flowing river.

Jose swung the boat in a big, scary turnaround to allow us to dock going against the current. To try to hit shore going downstream would cause the bow to hit shore, the stern to swing out and probably capsize us. Turned around, we edged upstream toward shore. When the bow touched, Victor plunged his long, hand-carved oar, with a rope attached, into the mud bank. The river current kept the boat against the bank.

Bill stood up in the boat, wiggling as he balanced. I was wondering how he would make that big step from boat to the muddy shore. We did it as we learned the "stepping-ashore-in-mud" technique, which is the most important of all river ballet steps, usually learned the hard way. If you neglect to take great care, the first footstep in the mud tends to slide back down toward the water. If you react to that by bracing your other leg against the boat, which is natural instinct, you push the boat away and perform an awkward, but memorable, splits, followed by a face-down "splat" in the mud, clawing fingers into the bank to keep from sliding under the boat. You might even excite the eager audience of piranhas in their muddy front-row seats. (Olympic judges might award you 0 to 3, depending on how gracefully you stuck the landing. The degree of difficulty helps a little). That's when you stop worrying about your new mud facial and wet clothes and start clawing up the bank to get your body parts out of the river.

From personal experience, our guess was that a person fails this only once. The taste and feel of mud are hard to forget. That first step out of the boat is the critical move. It has to be solid.

Later in the trip when we had mastered our modes of transport, Bill pointed out that as baseball little leaguers we might have dreamed of making the majors someday but, as a consolation, back home we might lay claim to being the two greatest "Pickup Truck Riding, Pecke-Pecke Mudbank Disembarkers" in the States, maybe even in the world.

Jose then led us on a walk through this lower level of the selva, which was land below the water level during the rainy season, and we looked at the trees, which had been flooded half the time to a level about a foot above our heads. It is quiet darkness under the canopy of thick trees. The jungle above the flooded area is virtually impassable. Vines grow on all the trees, underbrush of all kinds tangle and form a green wall that has to be cut through by teams of machete-wielding men to make any passageway at all. I couldn't help thinking about how slow early overland exploration must have been.

Bill punched me in the shoulder and said, "Hammer, there aren't any trees here that I know. No oaks, elms, pines, not even palms or anything we have at home. I don't even see any Florida stuff."

"Yeah, even the bushes and vines are different. See that jungle mess on the higher land? You couldn't cut your way through that stuff. It's like a solid plant wall."

Capitan Victor brought up the rear. In the trees, just above the high-water level, stood large termite nests made of mud, about basketball size, where the termites lived during the flooded season. From these nests intricate mud tubes led down the tree trunk to the ground—tunnels for their travel to the ground in the drier season. Strangely, both large and small termites lived in the same colonies.

Without a close inspection, termites and ants look the same to me. South America is famous for its thousands of species of both. The organization and collective works of these insects are prodigious. The only reason I can imagine for those long tubes they make from their nests to the ground would be to prevent being picked off by flying predators, like hungry birds or spiders. I'm sure the tubes are dissolved by the seasonal rising river water. Why don't they live on high ground all year? All they eat is wood, and there is plenty of it higher up.

Bill drew his big knife and hacked at a few small trees on the hike, a practice he would continue on every stop. He was always giving new trees a whack test. Except for the growing blisters on his feet he was developing from his new combat boots, he loved walking through the jungle. What he would have liked more was to unpack his fishing rod and do some casting. There had been no chance so far.

Jose came back to us from up ahead to give us a fruit that looked like a large orange but was green. It was not a grapefruit. I looked at the smiling Jose, "Naranja?" He had a mouthful of his but shook his head no. "Pomelo?" I asked. He kept shaking his head. OK, so it wasn't an orange or grapefruit.

When he had half swallowed his mouthful, Jose spurted out, "Citrus!" an outburst showering us with a generous spray of his half-chewed fruit.

Oh, great, we still didn't know what they were. We ate them anyway. They tasted like a combination of the two, but as much as I have tried, since returning from this trip, I cannot find out what they really were. I guess they were "citruses," like Jose said.

One of the major disappointments on this trip had raised its ugly head already: the inability of our guides to explain their environment. No names for trees or foliage of any kind and none for birds or bugs. They couldn't explain anything, even in Spanish. I would ask," Como se dice," or "Qual es el nombre," "Como se llama?" or anything else that might bring out something, but I usually got some unintelligible local name, a grunt, or a shoulder shrug. It would have been quite different if we had been with an educated bi-lingual professional guide.

Well, there weren't any in this part of the world. Where was Fearis when we needed her?

In our run-up to this expedition, I admit being a little lazy in looking for background material, but I did look for field manuals of birds, trees, and other wildlife and was amazed that even National Geographic, with great manuals on other parts of the world, had nothing to offer on Amazonia. I suppose this tells us that this forest region of our planet, which drains an area as large as all of Europe and is estimated to be inhabited by half of all the world's living species, is not sufficiently studied for publication. Of course, that makes it all the more intriguing. I was hoping to be with a knowledgeable guide, but we weren't, so we would have to collect our own questions and take them home.

That brought up the thought of how Fearis might have conducted this trip if she were here. There wasn't room for her in this boat or the tents. It just made us wonder if she had ever done this before herself. She, her tent and provisions would never have fit in this boat. Maybe she couldn't answer those questions either and decided to send us off with these two guys and tell us how easy they were to talk to when she, in fact, had never tried to talk to them in English.

Back in the boat after our first hike, we traveled a couple more hours around some large bends in the river. It widened and we seemed to be slowing. Late in the afternoon the sun was lowering and flickered through the leaves, as we moved. The river was a tawny hue as we floated along the east shore. Victor swung the boat around and we tied up facing upstream on the west shore.

Several times our passing had alarmed interesting birds. Some I knew from similar shore species in Florida; most I had never seen. There was a pair in particular that seemed strange. They flew overhead and landed somewhat awkwardly in the leafy branches of overhanging limbs that didn't seem sturdy enough for birds of their size, and bounced up and down from the impact. Two more sort of crash-landed near them. They were about the size of pheasants. They seemed to be trying to keep just out of sight behind leaves but not far away. As one looked at me, I could see only its head. The eyes were bright red, surrounded by a patch of blue skin, and there was a tuft of rumpled brown feathers on top of his head like a Mohawk haircut that needed trimming. It seemed that as we came closer, they wouldn't fly away. Instead, they crawled out of our sight, climbing and shuffling deeper into the leaves. I had never seen birds like these, either in person or in my dad's big John James Audubon book that I used to look through. I was going to ask our guides about them later when we got off the river for the night.

We unloaded the boat and started to make camp for the night. Victor had selected a gently sloping hill, which put us above the high-water level in a wooded area. Victor and Jose went about their work of putting up two small tents and building a fire in an open area, not far from the tents.

Like a rustic Martha Stewart, Jose then demonstrated the way he would make our daily drinking water. He scooped a kettle full of the muddy river water and put it over the fire until it began to boil. He then took it off the fire, put it on some flat surface and covered it with a lid of some kind. In the morning we would see the results.

We ate our fried bananas with some provisions Victor had dished up and finished off the rest of the water from the plastic gallon jug. From then on, we would have to drink Jose's river-water creation. We did not know what we would do if we gulped and found a live (or dead) animal in our mouths.

I started asking some questions about what lay ahead for us and began to realize that our Japanese-looking leader spoke no English or Japanese; even I could tell that Jose, who spoke no English, spoke lousy Spanish also, or maybe a dialect. The answers I received were a bit curt and the facial expressions were saying that they can't explain it but they know what they are doing and you will see.

Bill and I crawled into our small, two-man tent that did have an attached canvas floor, which would be nice to have on some of the damp camping areas or if we parked on some critters by accident. They have more species of ants than the rest of the world combined, plus little poisonous frogs, and a lot of termites and who knows what else. "Sweet dreams, Guillermo."

Too hot to crawl into a sleeping bag, we slept in our clothes, using our sleeping bags as a mattress. We slept in opposite directions. Amazingly, it turned out that neither of us kicked the other in the face, neither uttered nightmarish screams, and I had to crawl out for relief only once a night in those days. Bill was a great guy to travel with; never crabby or demanding, accommodating, did more than his share of the work and never complained about my snoring. I was lucky. He was also able to draw upon his "cave dweller" vocabulary to concoct new entertaining swear words to suit new inconveniences as we ran into them.

The night was calm, hot and humid but cooled after sundown just enough to cause the heavily laden air to condense and constantly drip from the trees overhead. As Yogi Berra, the great meteorologist, once said, "It ain't the heat, it's the humility."

I reached into my duffel and grabbed my little notebook with the stubby golf course pencil stuffed down the rings and started to catch up on how we got here and what was interesting. No problem in the dark—just prompts to remind me of the events that I could chronicle later.

I guess that I was the genetic or designated family historian. I hear there is always one. I made a habit of writing up the stories when I took strange new trips, putting them into handwritten letters to my mother, who also enjoyed writing and saving things like that. It was also a break from my business career of writing memos and reports—those clear-cut epistles written in a way so that they "cannot be misunderstood," devoid of editorial opinion and humor. It is difficult to learn, especially for someone who tends to be a smartass in the first place, but I managed to be good at it. That discipline, however, made writing these travel letters kind of a vacation. I could make any old observation I wanted. It was like I could virtually fart in church or laugh at a funeral, with impunity, maybe even applause.

Mosquito netting with a zipper closed each end of the tent. I proudly developed a quick exit maneuver that let in almost no mosquitoes. With a flashlight in my mouth, I unzipped the tent, pushed out on my back, using elbows and heels, and when my head was outside the tent, I reached back with both hands, pulled back and up to a sitting position, zipped it closed and got on my way. Stumbling back from my short hike, I reversed the move and slid back in, smacked any hitch-hiking mosquitoes and went back to sleep. Bill never woke up.

Chapter 7

Deadly Air Attack

Just before sunup, that time when the eastern sky is just showing some light, a chicken crowed somewhere deep in the woods. "Chickens?" Bill growled. "Where did we camp, in some barnyard?"

We weren't near anything like that, just jungle. "Where were they from?" I wondered aloud. "Could they be wild?" After thinking about it, I started to wonder where chickens came from in the first place, and I didn't mean eggs. Surely, they were once wild before they were domesticated, but where? Of all the chickens I had seen and raised when I was a kid on the farm, I never once questioned their wild ancestry. I knew that Rhode Island Reds were small, but so was the state of Rhode Island. I never gave that much thought either. I could not remember ever hearing anyone mention hunting wild chickens. They were farm animals and that's all. But, these were feral fowl. Had they escaped and gone back to wild, red jungle fowl? Or did they always live here in the jungle?

We never would find out. In fact, we never really saw them, just heard them.

Jose made some strong black coffee. Bill didn't have any. Then Jose, with a little flourish and a touch of jungle smugness, took the lid off the kettle of boiled, muddy river water from the night before and we were all eyes. He was about to display the finished product of his freshwater project that we would have to depend upon for the duration of this trip. We could see in the kettle that the mud had settled to the bottom; the mud portion made up about one third of the kettle. Jose then scooped out the clear water (well, semi-clear) and funneled it into the plastic jug with a self-congratulating glance at us, as if to say, "See, you doubting gringos, I told you I know what I'm doing." We smiled and let him enjoy his triumph.

While we munched on some papaya, bananas and burnt toast, I asked them what those birds were that kept crawling around in the limbs, with their red eyes and feathers sticking up on their heads. They didn't seem to know, or care. Jose just shrugged and held his nose, like he smelled something.

I asked about the chickens here in the wild and where they came from and got about the same amount of information. They looked at each other as if I had just asked where God came from. They merely told us that they are here. They live in this jungle. "Viven aqui, la selva, si."

You just can't beat having a couple of really well-prepared, knowledgeable and experienced tour guides to enlighten and educate curious newcomers. On the other hand, they were creating a lasting experience to write about or look up when we got home, assuming we made it home.

We brushed our teeth using a cup of the newly cleansed water, poured fresh from the filthy plastic jug, and packed up our gear. The tents were rolled and stowed and we were on our way, still early in the morning. The river meandered, dividing around islands just the same as yesterday. It was about 11:00

AM before we made our first stop. This was going to be a hike through low forest, below the high-water level. The going was easy with little underbrush.

Movies, like the old Tarzan movies, may have made us believe that the jungle was alive with the sound of screeching, swinging monkeys or whistling birds and, perhaps, a lion's roar echoing through the woods. On the contrary, it is a hushed, still place with the thick vegetation killing most distant sounds. It feels as muted as walking through a clothes closet. There are certainly animals capable of making noises, but they are rare and spaced, mostly freezing in place with curiosity when some strange intruder is walking through.

It became hotter as we moved deeper through this vegetable humidor. Jose had gone ahead of us and Victor was bringing up the rear. Bill had hardly whacked more than four trees when Victor shouted some kind of warning. All I could pick out was his screaming "Cuidado! Cuidado!" We could see Jose up ahead, standing on a limb of a tree, pounding on an immense termite nest with a stick.

Then we saw it break open with an explosion of BATS! The thing was full of bats. Gray darts flew all around us in jerky patterns—real, live, rat-like creatures with wings. A couple of them, not yet airborne, approached Jose on the tree. Couldn't he see them? That nest Jose was battering wasn't a termite home, at least not any more. It may have been built by the termites but it was now full of bats. Was he nuts?

Bill and I flailed our arms wildly, ducking, gyrating like idiots and trying to look everywhere at once. They moved so fast that you could not focus on them. They were just brown streaks or specks. The thought that one might hit you and bite was the real fear. We thrashed around to avoid looking like anything that a bat would want to land upon or bite. Then we ducked down in as low a spot as we could find and tried to hide.

Jose, you dumbass.

It eventually calmed down. They seemed to be gone. We sat, exhausted, sweat soaked, but wary, probably yelling a few more epithets to our brilliant crew, Jose. This was the same Jose that was sitting at the table when that person told us that sixty people in the area had just died from being bitten by rabid bats. If he was really trying to kill us, he must have been a bit suicidal also. Was he afraid that the river water he was forcing us to drink wouldn't really get the job done?

Luckily, the bats seemed to be settled somewhere. Soaked with sweat and battered by limbs and leaves while bobbing and weaving through the underbrush, we used every swear word we could remember as we stumbled our way back to the boat. No bites. Jose was still shaking his head. He didn't know there were bats in that nest, and he felt stupid.

He was. No argument. It might have been funny if we hadn't heard about the rabid bats and the death toll, but we weren't laughing.

We hoped he knew more about steering this boat than he did about wrecking termite nests with a club. Victor seemed to have some doubts too, because he took over the rudder and sent Jose up to the bow.

No telling why they really switched positions or, for that matter, why they did most things. Our concern was more with the little pecke-pecke motor staying functional for a couple of weeks. We sat in the boat, binge-eating Brazil nuts, swearing quietly about the crew, and watching the jungle. Our confidence in the expedition leadership waned by the hour.

We continued downstream for a couple more hours without much conversation. That might have been a close call. Dying of rabies in Puerto Maldonado was not part of our plan. We would have to keep an eye on Jose.

It was clear from the long turns and loops we were making that traveling this river took approximately ten miles of river travel to cover a distance of two or three miles as the crow flies. If Puerto Maldonado was a little over 100 miles from the Bolivian border we would probably have to travel somewhere between 250 to 300 river miles to reach it.

The river could take on many shades of brown, depending on the lighting. As our little boat passed close to a bank with tall trees shading the water, it began to take on a bronze color. In the late afternoon the sun reflected off a smooth surface like a gold disk. For two hours more we cruised downstream, around other islands, stopping only once more before making camp in an elevated forest of larger trees. A lone native passed our location, silently floating downstream in a dugout. He raised a paddle. Jose raised his hand. That was all the traffic we saw on the river for these three days.

I learned, from some reading, that the Indians indigenous to this area were the Ese Ejja. Like everything in Peru, they were known by several names: Chama, Ese Eja, Ese Exa, Huarayo, Guarayo and Tiatinagua people—and they settled by the tributaries of the Inambari, Tombopata and Heath rivers that flowed from the mountains. They weren't camped near here. I understood that their history of cannibalism was just old lore. They had been warlike in the old days but were now settled down to hunting, fishing, plus gathering Brazil nuts and honey. We hoped.

British explorer, Colonel Percy Harrison Fawcett, and the unsolved mystery of his disappearance along with his son and entire party, has been made quite famous since he was friends with adventure writers Arthur Conan Doyle and Rider Haggard. Fawcett had made over seven previous trips to the Amazon valley, starting as a surveyor for Bolivia to map the Bolivian border with Peru in 1910, which is near where we were. Later, he took trips to Brazil in the Mato Grasso region in search of the "El Dorado" or the lost civilization of the Lost City of Z. In 1925 he went missing there, with his son, and there have been as many as thirteen expeditions to find him; over 100 people have died in the attempt, besides the many who died with Fawcett's long expeditions.

While on the earlier Heath river expedition in 1910, his party was attacked by these Huarayo Indians in a bow and arrow barrage. Fawcett was famed for approaching them, wading through the river, braving the arrows, waving a bandana until they stopped the assault. They met and became friendly. Not having learned this until long after our trip, we had no fear of hostile Indians—only insects, rabid bats, dirty water, piranhas, caimans and poisonous snakes. Just a picnic in the park.

The Huarayos lived an entirely subsistence life, completely on the resources of the jungle. That must be rare in the world today—no supermarkets, no hardware stores. It fascinated us to think about it. Hunting with homemade bows and arrows and fishing was for the men only. The women gathered berries and fruit and maybe small animals; the women also planted grain and ground it themselves, by hand, but it was the men who gathered the Brazil nuts and honey.

We wondered how this separation of chores had evolved. We had seen no sight or sign of them all day and for about eighty miles downstream. We felt very far from life as we had always known it, in both distance and time, and the strange realization that we couldn't do anything about returning to it any faster than it took to get here was a little unsettling. Every pecke pecke of the little motors took us deeper and farther. Neither of us discussed it much.

Late in the afternoon the sun was lowering. Sunlight flickered through the leaves as we moved. The river cast back a tawny hue as we floated along the east shore. Victor swung the boat around and, as before, we docked facing upstream on the west shore. We unloaded the boat to make camp for the night. He had again selected a gently sloping hill above the high-water level. Victor and his crew—the batty, bat-battering Jose—set up two tents, built a fire and then started to concoct a meal.

At dark Victor took his flashlight and said, "Mira, mira." He just smiled and held his flashlight at the riverbank below and we could see two dozen pairs of red lights in areas around the shore. They didn't move. It was hypnotic.

"Caiman," Victor explained, "por todos lados en el rio." They were the eyes of the South American alligators, called caimans, and he was telling us they were everywhere. We never saw even one along the banks during the day; yet they were everywhere. We decided to look a little more carefully the next day.

How about stepping on one of those by mistake?

As the fire died down, I tried to ask a few more questions about this trip and got some hard-to-understand answers. They did not try any English. Apparently, my few Spanish words made them think I knew more than I really did, and they decided it was better to use a little Spanish than their few English attempts. After that fruitless intercourse, we all went to our tents.

An eternal humming concert of mosquitoes reminded me of one of the millions of questions I would like to ask Noah about his ark cargo. Why a pair of mosquitoes? At least, why didn't you swat them when you finally docked at Arrarat?

The answer was clear to me. He didn't give a damn about bugs. He probably didn't have any of the Amazon animals. Well, at least these were not nearly as big, as loud, or as many as I had experienced one summer about thirty-six years before at Camp Kooch-i-ching in Rainy Lake on the Canadian–Minnesota border. Those vicious, bloodsucking monsters covered the mosquito netting and sounded like a squadron of B-29s. They made these little Amazon skeeters look like gnats. But they weren't gnats and they also liked drilling you too—a constant menace in these woods.

A tough old northwoods veteran and former Chicago Bears tackle, Bob Townley, once told me that you won't itch from mosquito bites if you just let them finish drawing out that stuff they first injected into you before sucking your blood, then let them fly away along with your blood.

Let them withdraw and fly away? It takes a hell of a lot of will power, however, to watch one of those things that drilled his snout in you swell up with your blood, withdraw and fly away. Swatting them as they go is fair game, if you're quick and don't mind the red splatter.

We hadn't had much sleep for a couple of nights so we had no trouble sleeping like logs in this weird new habitat. I went to sleep dreaming about bats, how we were going to make sure we kept Jose in sight at all times and never let him get his hands around another club or stick.

Victor said that tomorrow we will see something. "Vamos aver algo."

I had no idea what he meant.

Chapter 8

Ghost Ship

We traveled very far the next morning, stopping for one visit in the low jungle, an area that appeared to be flooded much of the year. We hiked a long distance this time, more than two miles from the boat. We only hoped that at least one of our two leaders knew where we were going and how to get back.

Bill hacked a few trees as usual. If we were ever lost, like Hansel and Gretel, we could follow the trail of hacked trees to return. Suddenly, as he casually took a chop at a tall, thin one with a smooth, silver colored trunk, it sounded surprisingly like a clank, not a chop, and he stopped. This thing was like iron. He had given it his normal hard whack, but his blade only scraped a little bark. It was about four inches in diameter and was the same thickness up to its top, which was about thirty feet. That's the way bamboo grows but this wasn't bamboo. Palm-like fronds grow only from the top. Its trunk was smooth, uniform in light gray color and thickness, without tapering, all the way to the top, devoid of any lower limbs or knots. It looked like an aluminum flagpole. It was hard, not like a palm, and had to be strong to grow that high, that thin and never be blown over and broken.

How does it grow that way? I wondered. Did it sprout fronds then use its photosynthesis to grow the trunk, pushing up the frond area to reach the canopy? It didn't even try to make limbs along the way—thirty feet of smooth, limbless trunk, measuring about four inches in diameter all the way. Someday, we hoped we would find out. Someday.

Victor knew the name of this tree, which I failed to write down, and later noted it as a hard, strong wood. It seemed to be a hardwood disguised as a palm. We did learn later that this heavy, stone-hard wood was used by the Indians to make bows and their arrowheads. The arrowheads were long, thin and had carved barbs for shooting fish.

Our two leaders led us deeply into the forest. Bill and I were soaked in perspiration, all the time fighting underbrush and vines. The forest that was nearest the river and remained a part of the flooded area during the rainy season remained relatively free of underbrush. The farther we went and the deeper into the forest, the more we gradually ran into more underbrush. We were in areas that the river had long abandoned and some elevated areas with the big trees, covered with every kind of vine imaginable, surrounded by competing species of trees, tangled, intertwined and too thick to even consider cutting through. It became obvious why explorers used the river systems and why clearing these forests, road building, farming and settling were nearly impossible. Trying to hack your way through the densest high ground would seem to take so long that it might grow in behind you. Biting, crawling insects of every kind seem to like it too. Swinging a machete with one hand might be less activity than swishing bugs away with the other.

Their Spanish word for this forest tangle was el infierno verde—green hell.

What could be worth running this gauntlet? We rested a couple of times, but that brought on some curious bugs, so we kept going. Occasionally, we heard some tree animal—either a bird, monkey or something—rustle, screech or whistle just to let us know they were around and watching. Just as we were about to ask some questions about this long ordeal, Jose stopped and pointed, "mirar por encima de alli!"

Through the trees and vines we could see what looked like the rusty metal skeleton of a large boat—a steamboat, right there in the thick forest. Its main wooden hull, all rotted away, still had most of its metal frame, rusted but still in place, along with the boiler, engine and remnants of a wooden deck. It was a ghost ship, covered with jungle. Small trees had sprouted and grown through it, vines clutched it. How could it be here?

It was slowly being eaten by the jungle.

Sweat-drenched and exhausted, Bill and I looked at each other for a minute with a new surge of energy. What was this? We had to get closer and climb on it if we could. It stood in a shallow stagnant puddle. The metal bow barely showed, about two feet above the puddle of water that surrounded it. The ubiquitous, tiny butterflies of every color fluttered around the puddle. We could walk onto the boat on the metal frame and access the engine and boiler section. The stack was still there, reaching about fifteen feet high. It had been galvanized so it survived the rusting of the rest. Our curiosity was in high gear. We looked over every manmade item on this wreck. The boiler bore a plate that read, "Mannheim 1936." We found instructions in German on a plate attached to another part of the boiler—obviously this was a German steamboat. It must have been, of course, a boat from the time of Nazi Germany and probably had been there for many years. But why? How? We were two miles from the main river.

That was spooky. Our guides, filled with their infinite knowledge of historic local lore, just shrugged their shoulders as usual. "No lo se, Señores. Allemania." They didn't know; they knew only that it was German.

It seemed, for some strange reason, this vessel lost power or strayed somehow away from the mainstream during the high-flood time, lodged in the trees and was abandoned. Why? I felt like Indiana Jones from the recent movies of the Lost Ark or some other quest. He usually got lost in some place filled with snakes and then had the inevitable confrontation with the Nazis and a narrow, acrobatic escape. I was always looking around for snakes anyway and there was no expectation of storm troopers, so we kept looking around.

This boat appeared to be some sixty or seventy feet long. What was a boat that large doing and where would it have been going? There were no major cities or industries to visit this far up the Madre de Dios. Was it going upstream for gold? Brazil nuts? No rubber was on board. The Amazon rubber boom had ended more than twenty years before this engine was built. The boat's name was nowhere to be found. Did it get swept away from a mooring during a flood? Was it hidden on purpose? Why had no one tried to salvage it?

Only the engine and rusting skeleton were left and there was no telling who knew anything about it, least of all, our captain and crew. Strangely, it seemed that this area was no longer even part of the annually flooded river forest. Even the dense vegetation was not that of the flooded river bed. We had hacked our way through much of it. The main flow, even at flood stage, had to be at least a mile or more from there.

We hiked back to our boat, watching out for termite nests discharging flying gray things, all the time keeping an eye on Jose—our tree-climbing, bat-battering buffoon—to make sure he didn't make another attempt on our lives. We reached our boat, climbed in, and moved on downstream. Our guides offered no explanation for the ghost ship. It had been there as long as they have visited here, and they hadn't been too sure where it was, judging by the zigzag route we took through the forest.

The hours of high sun were always quiet in the jungle. Few birds flew. No noises or jumping fish or swinging monkeys, no screeches. Things don't look alive until the hours between 4:00 and sundown. Nighttime is still and sultry, with no cooling breeze. Then, at the first bit of sunlight on the horizon in the morning, the jungle wakes up. The animals, particularly birds, must think they have just survived the end-of-the-world and are happily up and flying, chirping or squawking and looking for fun, food or sex and just following the flock leader to wherever he is taking them next. Later, when they are slowed down in the late morning and the heat is greatest, they roost again, stare around, sleep or digest their breakfast.

Victor knew the river and how to navigate it. He took the outside of bends, where the current was fastest. He seemed to be decisive about which branch of the stream to take around any island and gave clear orders to Jose in the bow when he needed him for some turning maneuvers to help with his long oar.

Bill worked as our spotter. He watched everything. He saw the first caiman and it was apparent why we had seen none the day before. They lie motionless, covered with mud, the same mud they are sitting in near the shore. Perfect camouflage. The only contrast they offered was when their mud covering was dry and lighter in color than the wet mud where they were basking.

Caiman are smaller than our alligators, reaching lengths of only about five feet. Alligators can be three times that length. Caiman still have very big mouths and somewhat longer teeth than gators. They have the same habit of sitting motionless for hours. We weren't going to pet them, but we were hoping to see one with the mud cleaned off.

Victor spotted a sheer cliff honeycombed with holes, parrots living in each of them. We stopped there for a look. It was a wall of the same brown color as the river but dotted with the bright green and red polka dots of the birds' bodies all lying in their holes. At first, they looked too small to be parrots. Closer, we could see that they were indeed large. Like other bird species, they look so much alike that you wonder how they tell each other apart.

We threw a rock at the cliff to stir up some action, maybe some flight, a cloud of brilliant colors to fill the sky, squawks, screeches—something. Nothing happened—maybe a flick of a wing or a dirty look, nothing else. I took a picture of the cliff that I knew anyone looking at it would say, "What is that?" Then we went on our way.

"I really want to go fishing, Hammer. Why can't I troll a line or something?" Bill asked as he looked around in his duffel for his collapsed three-piece rod and reel.

It was clear that my partner had seen enough muddy tree trunks, caiman and the backside of that little hunyak, Jose, in the bow. He was ready for some action. The hard wooden plank we sat on was not getting any more comfortable, and there was no leaning back to rest.

I turned around to our little Admiral to ask if Bill could fish, "OK, Capitan Victor, mi piscador quiere que piscar. Es posible?"

"No no, mas tardes o mañana, si?"

"Guillermo, he said maybe later or tomorrow, I think."

Victor then rambled on about our being in a fishing place with fishermen tomorrow, or something like that.

As the sun was now behind the trees, Victor took us down what you might call a rainforest "side street," a small tributary away from the main river that appeared to be a narrow, slow-moving stream. The jungle trees formed a picturesque canopy overhead, creating this peaceful tunnel into the trees. It was a perfect picture of a jungle stream—inviting, promising great new things to see. The flat water reflected the overhanging tree and the red sun. I had to take a photo. It was a nice break from the big river. I asked him what this was and he said it was Lago Valencia.

My map showed a large oxbow lake on the left side of the main river. It didn't show that it was still connected to the river by a small waterway.

The water was glassy smooth without any serious current, still murky like the river, yet a little easier to see objects just under the surface. Bill was itching to fish it.

An oxbow lake is formed by meandering rivers cutting its meander loop larger and larger over time while also cutting itself into a circle and cutting deeper at its start until it finally cuts through its own original stem, straightening itself and leaving the large bend as an isolated oxbow lake. Sometimes a flooding session can assist and hasten the cut-through. This lake still managed a small stream to the main river. Valencia was many miles long, curving far out of sight through the trees.

I remembered how this same kind of river erosion and oxbow cutoffs had complicated the state borders along the Mississippi River, which were originally set as the river's edge, only to have the river meander miles away from the state lines over the ensuing years, making life hell for map makers. The streams wandered but the state lines remained where originally mapped.

We floated along the bank for an hour and pulled over next to two or three native canoes near where the Indians camped up the hill. We made camp nearby while our crew did a lot of talking to the men, discussing fishing. They were all friendly and laughing. They seemed to speak a strange language, sharing knowledge and advice with Victor. I couldn't understand a thing I heard, but I could tell when Victor was explaining to them about the two of us. They were very curious and repeatedly looked over at us as he talked. I told Bill they were looking over at him because he is a foot taller than they are, he has that magnificent Cro-Magnon face, and he scares them.

Guillermo and Jose—shows size difference between
gringo "tourist" and native boat crewman.

Or maybe they are wondering how we would taste on their rotisserie. Historically, human flesh was known as part of their diets, albeit ceremonial in nature. Certainly, that was ancient history now. Right?

These men were native Huarayo tribe fishermen and this was their fishing camp, a long way from their permanent village, probably because this lake was good fishing, much better than the fast-moving river.

They had tents and a small shack, some dogs, cats, chickens and some kids, only a couple of women. They kept a fire going with the smoke blowing where we were going to sleep. They also had a latrine that was a community poop hole. It stunk so badly we could hardly breathe if the breeze blew toward us. I hoped our camp was far enough away and upwind.

They caught fish for days and without any type of refrigeration, keeping them the old-fashioned way, salted. They seemed to be in no particular hurry to run home. Victor told us that we were going fishing with them tomorrow. Great! Finally, a chance for Guillermo to unlimber his fishing rod and dazzle these locals.

These natives were not in loincloths, war paint or feathers. Their clothes were home tailored, classic "last year's rummage sale rejects." They had bare feet—something I was as likely to consider as pounding another termite nest. No doubt it was because their canoes were essentially curved logs, partly submerged as they paddled, sitting in their bilge puddle all day. They appeared to be wearing some things they had worn for months.

That evening we feasted on some freshly caught filet of Red Bellied Piranha, the local catch of the day that Chef Jose had obtained from the Huarayo anglers. Served with this fabulous, culinary fish entrée were the familiar, well-done banana hockey pucks, rice and some local fruit. In the candlelight we could not tell what the black dots were in the rice, so we waited to see if they moved before we poked a spoonful into our mouths.

The fish was not bad.

For dessert we indulged ourselves with our imported Walmartian Granola Bar and a sip of agua de Madres de Dios ala Jose, directly from this morning's kettle skimming. It was tolerable, but would have been better cold but, of course, cold anything was not part of this expedition.

The tent was as uncomfortable as usual but better after removing some lumps of hard dirt under the floor. In the tent, before falling off to sleep, we discussed the German ship for at least a half hour. We could have spent much more time there, but it had been a long hike from the boat. That ghost ship's untold story piqued the imagination, and the round-trip excursion through jungle had been no walk in the park. Dead sticks, vines, spider webs, and some prickly plants had to be dodged and, most importantly, you have to follow far enough behind your fellow trekker to be out of the backlash of some branches he has sprung aside.

We also had to stop and look up any time something rustled overhead. Birds drop nasty things and no one wants a stumbling, screeching monkey to fall on his head. Then there might be some odd fruit or pod that needs inspection. In Bill's case, of course, there was frequently something that needed whacking with the Rambo machete. Or maybe just a pee break.

We went over and over the only reasons we could think of that would put that steamboat there.

* * *

Some twenty-five years later, I uncovered stories of this ghost ship. While I was curiously researching developments in this Madre de Dios area since our visit there, I happened across an ad for a jungle lodge that talked about taking boat trips on the Madre de Dios River. To my complete surprise, one of the photos it displayed appeared to be the identical photograph of this skeleton steamship that I had taken so many years before. It was described as the wreck of the Contamana in which the legendary Carlos Fermin Fitzcarrald had died.

The infamous rubber baron was working up the Urubamba River in the 1880s and followed one of its tributaries to its source. He then climbed over a ridge and found another river flowing in the opposite direction, which he thought to be the source of the Purus River. Some of his native Indian workers had rumored that there was an Inca fort on the Purus guarding vast gold treasures. Fitzcarrald marked the spot where he landed and returned to Iquitos with his fortune in rubber.

Then in 1884 he came back to the spot in a ship named the Contamana. It is said that he brutally enslaved local natives to take apart the thirty-ton ship, move it overland and reassemble it on this river he thought was the Purus.

While exploring this river he was attacked several times by Indians and eventually ran into a group gathering rubber and returning to Bolivia. He then realized he was not on the Purus. He was actually on a river that flowed to the Manu river, then the Madre de Dios and on into Bolivia. Although it was the opposite direction from the Purus and the wrong river for him, he had actually made a major geographic discovery by finding a close link of the two main watersheds of the Amazon valley. That small ridge of land was all that existed between the two major river systems of the continent. This remote isthmus and a town nearby are named for him. Although his name was often associated with the founding of Puerto Maldonado, Carlos Fitzcarrald actually died in a whirlpool shipwreck in the Contamana on the Urubamba River in 1897, years before the founding of that town in 1902. He was thirty-five years old.

The tale of Fitzcarrald's life so fascinated movie producer Werner Herzog that in 1978 he decided to make a movie loosely based on his story. It starred Jason Robards and Claudia Cardinale with Mick Jagger as Fitzcarrald's sidekick. Shooting was in an area near Iquitos. After the movie was forty percent done, Robards got sick and Jagger went on a music tour. The tenacious and eccentric Herzog wouldn't quit. He replaced Robards with Klaus Kinski and started shooting all over again. He made Fitzcarrald into an eccentric Irishman named Brian Sweeney Fitzgerald. In the movie, Fitzgerald idolized Enrico Caruso and wanted to eventually bring opera to Iquitos. He spent a fortune winching a 30-ton vessel overland in one piece. (The original Fitzcarrald had sensibly taken it apart and reassembled it on the other side.) The ship in the film was named Molly Aida. The Aguaruna Indians helped in the film and six were injured. It took four long years to complete.

This film is "FITZCARRALDO." It is in German with Spanish subtitles. It actually earned many awards, including best director at Cannes, Germany Film prize, Golden Age and nomination for "Best Foreign Film" at the Academy Awards, and BAFTA.

I recently watched the movie. My conclusion: My photos of the ship appear to be the same as those claiming that it was the original wreck of the Contamana on which Fitzgerald— Fitscarrald? —was killed. There are other identical photos of the same wreck said to be the wreck of the movie ship, Molly Aida. This skeleton ship, now gradually being devoured by the forest, more than two miles from the main river, is too small to be the one in the movie.

However, ...

It is also highly unlikely that the real Contamana would have wrecked in 1892 using a steam engine built in Germany in 1936. Especially since this ghost is hundreds of miles from the Urubamba and in a different river system.

Since it is surely neither the Contamana nor the Molly Aida, we may never know what wreck it is. It is an unknown ghost ship that locals are determined to glamorize.

I would still like to know its story.

Chapter 9

Guillermo – Master Fishing Instructor

Thanks to some chickens that decided to sleep about two feet from our tent, we were up at about 4:00 AM. It seems that life without electricity—but with alarm chickens—tends to be a sunup-to-sundown existence. (Or, like Yogi said, "It gets late early out here.")

Without showers or baths for a while in this tropical climate, Bill and I probably wouldn't have passed the smell test in the locker room of a German gym team. Today, some time, we were determined to wash in the river, mud and all.

Bill was chafing at the bit to go fishing this morning, finally fishing in the Amazon Valley—catching big pintados, dorados, piranhas, paiche and the giant, air breathing anapaima. He had his rod and reel ready for the morning except for rigging the leader, lure or hook on the line. We first needed to see what sizes the locals were using. I hadn't brought a rod and was depending on the locals to supply whatever we needed. Besides, I was hoping to have a chance to shoot a bow and arrow at some fish if I could get the natives to let me try. I'd always heard that they did that in the Amazon.

After the usual breakfast, enhanced this time with a little of my imported Skippy chunk-style peanut butter I had been hiding deep in the duffel, we were on our way to the boats and fishing. The natives were out in the water in a couple of places, not far from shore. They had one boat that was larger than their canoes and could hold several fishermen, their nets and their harvest.

There was really no such thing as "sport fishing" in this jungle. All the fishing in the jungle rivers was for predator fish that live in muddy water and feed in a frenzy when some troubled or vulnerable fish or animal is detected. A really big frenzy will bring enough fish to throw a net. They also use poles (sticks) about six feet long with about six feet of steel wire. On it is a hook baited with a piece of red meat, the bloodier the better. They throw it in the water and wait for a bite. If it isn't taken immediately, they smack the water to imitate a feeding frenzy and attract those who can't see the bait through the muddy water.

When the fish hit, they hit hard, jerking away to protect their mouthful. The fishing skill is in pulling a hooked piranha, kicking and snapping, into the boat and unhooking it without having it catch you with its mouth full of razor blades. Red bellied piranhas were the native fish and reached about fourteen inches in length, with strong, thick bodies. We took a good, close look at the teeth of one and discovered it had what looked like a cluster of thin, white, pointed chisels where fangs or cuspids would be.

After a few minutes of preparation, the nearby Indians had a chance to see this tall, Wyoming cowboy-sport fisherman and his strange gear

Our new Huarayo buddies were watching, wide-eyed, as Bill readied his rod and reel. I am sure that they had never seen such a thing. We all watched as Bill pulled some line from the reel and threaded it through the guides on the rod, pulling an extra length through the tip so that he could tie on a length of leader. He then took off about four feet of leader from the spool, cut it and tied on a hook to one end using a hook that resembled those the natives were using. Jose then handed him a piece of red meat, which Bill carefully positioned so that the hook's barbed point was not showing.

By now the natives' boat was close enough to see Bill's every move. There were about eight of these weather-beaten Huarayo Indians pulled up close enough to quietly and meticulously study this skilled American sportsman's demonstration. Bill, perhaps feeling a little pressure in front of this awe-stricken crowd, casually tossed the hooked bait and leader in the water and quickly turned his attention to the reel and the setting of the drag so that he would be ready when there was a strike.

There were a couple of muffled oohs from the onlookers, then some aahs and a moan from the crowd, then a snicker, followed by a breakout of full bodied Huarayoan laughter when they realized what they had just seen. Bill looked up from his reel, suddenly realizing that he had not tied the leader to his line. The four feet of leader, hook and bait were out in the coffee colored water of Lago de Valencia all on its own. Bill was left holding his rod and reel and trying his best, I am sure, to think how he might keep me from telling this story back home.

That was impossible, of course.

When I could finally stop laughing that night, I also assessed him a fine of 500,000 Peruvian Intis for that debacle. The fine would have been greater, but for the mitigating factor of the lasting pleasure it brings me, just thinking about it.

We both then started fishing the native way, but Bill later tried his rod and reel so he could cast away from the boat. It's quite a jolt those fish put on the line when they yank that bait. They hate being caught and fight fiercely to get off the hook.

Properly tied up this time, Bill cast his line away from the frenzy, hoping to catch something different. He suddenly did snag a very heavy fish. He was fighting a losing battle to reel it in. The natives said it was a pintado, a fish that can grow to 200 pounds. They usually hibernate in hiding places when the river is not in flood stage. Bill must have had his bait sink and one of them decided to have a little snack and grabbed it. Bill fought it for a while, couldn't make any headway, and tightened the drag. It finally broke the line. Bill's tackle was too light for any kind of fishing in this neighborhood.

Neither of us had any prior knowledge on how to fish here from our trip advisor, Fearis, so we blamed it on her.

Mid-morning, we headed back to camp for siesta, fish cleaning and lunch. There, just as I had hoped, stood a native using a bow and arrow at the shoreline, and he was good at it. I observed him draw back a long arrow with its wooden barbed point, aim and zing. He missed. The arrow floated up, so he didn't lose it. He tried again and this time speared right through a good-sized fish.

With this long arrow through it, the fish wiggled off shore a little, but it was retrieved by a boy in a little dugout. The archer then offered me a chance to shoot one—just what I was hoping. I had a funny flashback of my childhood backyard games when I realized that a real Indian was actually giving me his bow and arrow to shoot. I almost did a little war dance.

I took the arrow, the stance, gripped the bow and tried to fit the bowstring in the notch at the back of the arrow. Their arrows didn't have notches, just flat ends. That was a surprise. The arrows sported only two feathers at the end, not three. The arrows are made of hollow, very straight reeds, which are buoyant. They were also twice as long as I expected. I got ready and started looking for a fish near the surface. Some within my sight were moving around but they wouldn't sit still. I knew all about refraction of light in the water and that the fish is always deeper than it looks. I took aim, let fly—missed. But, so had he, so I tried again—missed again. A third time, I was absolutely not going to miss. I waited, I saw a bigger fish than the last. I waited with the bow flexed and ready. My target slowed to a stop about a foot below the surface. Zap, I let fly... Missed again.

My smiling partner, Guillermo, the game fishing king of the lake, had his turn to laugh, which he did and also fined me 500,000 Intis. We were even, sort of. I thanked the little archer and left for a lunch of Brazil nuts and jerky in a carefully selected place—upwind from the poop hole.

Strolling later down where the fishermen were filleting the fish and throwing the bones and guts back into the water, we were treated to a frenzied cleanup crew of piranha swarming. Around some parked canoes we saw a young girl sitting in a log canoe with a knife, attempting to filet a piranha. It wasn't quite dead and she was having trouble as it kicked while she was holding it. At one kick it snapped and bit her finger, nearly taking off the tip of it. She bravely made not a peep, tried to stop the bleeding with a dirty old rag, and tried to act as if nothing important happened. It was bleeding profusely. That is when it dawned on us that we really didn't have much of a first aid kit. At least if there was one, we forgot to check it out. Victor was not around. She was finally helped by one of the men, probably her father. We hoped they had some antiseptic and that she had at least learned to cut the head off a piranha first, before doing any surgery on it. Why was she even on this trip?

Down by the water's edge I saw one of the fishermen sitting on his haunches in a way that only they and many Asian people can manage comfortably. You don't have to be an anthropologist to see the similarity between the native people in Peru and Asian people, in their physical characteristics: wide faces, large cheekbones, narrow eyes, darker skin color, and straight black hair sticking straight out from the scalp. They have brown eyes and, most noticeably, long torsos in relation to the length of their shorter legs. That kind of physical proportion allows them to squat with feet flat on the ground, lean slightly forward and have their center of gravity out far enough to be well balanced. They can sit that way for hours. As a catcher when playing baseball, I always envied that ability. A man of opposite build, like my long-legged partner Guillermo, with the shorter torso, would fall straight backward if he tried that. I have seen men in China and other Asian countries sitting like that for hours; but never in the long-legged countries in Africa, Europe or the U. S.

There is little doubt that they came to the North and South American continents on the land bridge or by boat in the Ice Age. I still can't figure out why some stopped in Alaska and the Yukon to live like Eskimos. Maybe they had a taste for blubber. Why not keep on going to California? I guess a few came down to this place.

Watching the men working near the water's edge, cleaning fish, working on poles, lines and nets, I saw that one man had a line that he was dragging slowly out of the water with a five-foot-long yellow and brown eel hooked on it. The thing had a wide, ugly face and some long, wavy brown fins on its side. It was an electric eel. I understand that they are actually fish but known as electric eels. Standing next to this eel sniggler was another man paying no attention, deeply occupied with some net repair. The sniggler looked at me, raised an eyebrow that gave me the sign and a wink that, in any language, says, "Hey! Watch this."

He quickly grabbed the ankle of the man next to him and at the same time clamped his hand on the electric eel. The unsuspecting man let out a big yelp and nearly did a full back flip. It was a beautiful Fosbury Flop, landing on his back. Even the Olympic high jumper himself would have been proud.

We couldn't help roaring with laughter. The prankster had actually let the full electrical shock of the fish go through him just to jolt his buddy and was laughing so hard you could see all three of his teeth at once.

It was great to know that even Huarayo braves have a good sense of humor.

That was actually a high price to pay for a laugh. I dearly wanted to pull the same thing on Bill, but I wasn't about to touch that eel.

Electric eels are known to send out a mild jolt to stun their prey before pouncing on them, but when threatened, they can shoot a big voltage charge into their attacker strong enough to stop a man's heartbeat. I wasn't in an experimental mode.

We were wondering if sometime tonight we would get to see Huarayo natives having a go at some of their legendary, visionary brew at an ayahuasca drinking ceremony, hallucinating about fighting big animals or their future lives after death. Apparently, they don't take their important shamans on fishing trips. The shaman is that especially skilled person with the ability to mediate between the living and dead, and interpret dreams. He probably occupies a status above fisherman and waits back at their village, with the women. We expected to visit an Indian village some time later.

Just when we thought we were going to spend another night here, Captain Victor began to pack up and load the boat. We pushed off at about 3:30 that afternoon and headed out of the lake, enjoying the calm tunnel through the trees on the way back to the main river. It was peaceful and relaxing. I took some photos that I knew were going to turn out well.

Bill said, "You suppose our little captain thought we had embarrassed him enough for one trip and got our asses out of there before we did something really stupid?"

"I don't know, maybe he doesn't like sleeping that close to the poop hole any more than we do."

"You aren't going to tell anyone about me not tying on that leader, are you?"

"Oh, come on, Billy, you know I wouldn't think of it. We don't have any way to tell anyone anything right now. I'll probably forget all about it in a few...years.... Ha." My jaws were sore from grinning. "What's it worth to keep quiet about that, Guillermo?"

Silence.

"You weren't so f*****g good with that bow and arrow, either, Robin Hood."

"Well, yeah...but you were just lucky I didn't grab you and that electric eel. And I would have, but I was just afraid I'd have to carry your big dead ass all the way back to the States. And what was I going to tell Sue?"

In spite of any discomforts we might have been enduring, we had our laughs doing it, and more to come.

Just before our pecke-pecke merged again with the main stream, Bill said, "Here come your dumb lookin' jungle pheasants again."

Above our canopy were two of those red-eyed, multi-colored, awkward birds sort of parachuting into the trees using their wings and wide-spreading tail to break their descent.

The limbs bounced with their weight. They scrambled through the leaves just out of our sight. I am convinced they had a keen but wary curiosity about us. Two more plunged in, a little farther from us. I no longer wondered if they were following us. I was sure they were.

Jose passed forward the bags of Brazil nuts and got our attention. He was trying to tell us something about the birds. He was pointing and holding his nose and making a face as if he was still downwind from the Indian poop hole. We thought he was having another brain fart like when he battered those bat nests.

* * *

It wasn't until months later, when I had looked everywhere to try and identify these crazy birds from my photos, that I discovered what they actually were and realized what crazy Jose was telling us. Those birds were the peculiar and unique hoatzins, also known as "stinkbirds." I had the strange feeling that I owed our little Batman back there a long overdue apology. Neither of them knew them by name, only by reputation.

The hoatzin is a folivore or leaf eater. It scarfs down lots of leaves and it has a huge gullet where fermentation takes place, just like cows. They are well known to smell like cow manure. Taxonomists have spent decades trying to relate them to other animals, finally deciding that they are their own avian family. A flock of these awkward flying cows can come in, strip a tree of its leaves and move on.

The newly hatched stinkbirds have claws on their wings and can use them to crawl through limbs before ever learning to fly. As a fashion statement, the hoatzin's color selections and plumage resemble a kindergarten kid that dressed himself in the dark. In one reference book, a British ornithologist described it best as "thrift shop chic." There is no hint at what Mother Nature had in mind.

Hoatzins have red eyes. Around their eyes are large circles of featherless, light blue skin. Their heads are small and have tall, tan feathers with black tips arranged in a messy Mohawk hairdo or maybe a sloppy Trojan warrior's helmet. The folded wings are dark brown with white feathers here and there; the undersides and belly feathers are reddish brown. It has a tail that can spread widely and is made of strawberry blonde feathers. The legs and claws are gray. Its cape-like wings with their claws make people think they are more closely related to dinosaurs than to plumed and groomed birds.

* * *

I knew nothing of this bird at the time but was filled with curiosity about them and their habits as we moved downstream. I was convinced they were following us and spying on us in their quirky and awkward way. Even though they were known locally for their cow-manure smell, we actually never smelled them. There were enough other jungle odors to go around. The birds that really remind you that you are in the jungle are the whistling pihas that sound like some smartass guys whistling at some girl across the street. "Wheeetwheuuu." The macaws make an opposite noise that blasts you with ear-piercing squawks that could wake the dead.

An hour downstream, through dense forest and around a vine-covered island on an elevated area on shore, some natives hailed us. Jose answered. We pulled over and stopped. Victor turned and asked us if I wanted to buy some tapir meat. "Quiere comprar carne de tapir?" The men had killed a big tapir in the jungle and were selling the meat. A bloody, black haired carcass lay there surrounded by some blood-covered Huarayo natives staring at their butchered mess of body parts. Flies buzzed about. It looked like a dead pony. Its severed head lay a few feet away, eyes open. It was like a long-nosed horse's head, like someone crossbred a pony and an anteater.

Victor looked at me expectantly. I had no answer. How would I know if we wanted tapir steaks? How old was it? Was it even edible? Not our call. Neither of us had ever really considered ourselves especially skilled as tapir meat buyers at riverbank auctions.

After further discussion with the butchers, Victor finally explained to me that it was all gone except for the head so he had taken the liberty of telling them "no gracias." We smiled at the thought of Victor thinking he had really saved us from an agonizing decision.

Bill reminded me, "I guess we aren't in Kansas anymore, Toto." And our yellow brick road was wet and muddy. We climbed back into our pecke-pecke riverboat and continued downstream. A crimson sun was gradually sinking behind us, making little Jose's shadow on the water in front of us, longer and longer.

We were a very long and worrisome way from Puerto Maldonado.

We pulled over at dusk, hauled everything up a steep hill and camped in a wooded area on the brink of a steep cliff over a tributary creek. Bill and I usually helped set up tents and gather wood, but this day we were determined to wash up. By now my hair was stiff with a week of dried sweat. The crew set up the tents. We both had decided, on our first day across the equator, to suspend shaving until we returned home. Here we were now standing in the muddy water, gradually sinking ankle deep in the mud bottom, soaping up and then pouring buckets of muddy water over our heads. That might seem a bit self-defeating, but the swap of old sweat for muddy water is still a good trade. We gave little thought to piranhas taking nips at our feet, but no problems.

Dinner was a fresh piranha filet, rice and a banana hockey puck, washed down with a cup or two of boiled and skimmed river water and "citrus" for dessert. "My kingdom for some ice." I never thought I would ever miss it so much.

It had been a long, full day. We were all weary and trying to cool off. While Chef Jose was boiling tomorrow's kettle of river water, I wondered, for a minute, what animals had peed upstream from Chef Jose when he filled the kettle. Well, it would still be considered "organic" back home, wouldn't it?

After a day of sitting on the boat plank unsupported, I found a spreading, wing-like root on a giant kapok tree that just suited the curve of my tired back, so I sat back, relaxed, pulled out a pocket knife and started carving. I had always loved to carve things as a kid. Thoughts about this trip were running through my head. Having a bucket list of things we want to do is a natural thing. Who hasn't said, "Someday I'd love to..."? Even though Bill and I had different careers, this rainforest was one of the strong curiosities we shared. At this point, though, I wondered if we hadn't overcooked this one. For the last sixteen years I had traveled internationally about half the time. Such travel had its own set of discomforts, like fighting constant jet lag at home, being out of touch, with piles of mail awaiting and the long hours working it down, totally out of sync with the kids' activities, sports teams and local news. Hotels and new beds get old; in many countries, so does the food. In countries like India, Indonesia and Mexico, food can have some interesting side effects that make working uncomfortable.

On the other hand, I realized that in most cases I was flying in business or first class, eating in some of the best of the local eateries and riding around in nice cars with interesting people. After a few years, I had learned some tricks that helped: like telling people in one country that I was leaving on Friday and the people at the next stop that I would arrive on Monday. That gave me a couple days to be on my own at a destination so I could avoid bothering people who might feel obligated to entertain me, avoid more cathedral visits, see something that I wanted to see and catch up a little on paper work.

We hit the sack early. No fireside chats or marshmallow roasts. Of course, "Hitting the sack" was purely a cliché referring to the idea of going to sleep for the night and bore no resemblance to our real-life partial stripping off dirty, worn clothes, sliding into the zippered corner of our three-foot-high tent without kicking one's tent mate in the face and then testing the ground under the sleeping bag for lumps from rocks, sticks or animals. Once in, we were looking at the feet of the other, trading a potential of banana breath for smelly feet. A flashlight was nearby, Bill's survival knife within grasp, a smaller one near me. My head was near the zippered corner.

Bill and I usually had some discussion of the day's happenings and this evening was no exception. I decided to bring up a subject that had been wearing on me since we pushed off from the little mud pier at the Puerto Maldonado marina.

"Guillermo, I have been looking at our map. It's not a great map. Not a lot of detail, but one thing that is bothering me is that we don't have a destination. We don't have a predetermined place to jump out and go home by car, train or airplane. We are going downstream and away from our little entry to this rainforest. There isn't much downstream on this map. Every one of our pecke peckes downstream will require several peckes to push us back upstream. We are totally reliant on that noisy little motor to fight the current and return upstream. When the little admiral decides to return, we are going to make that four miles per hour boost we get from the current into a four miles per hour pushback. We lose about eight miles per hour just by turning toward home. I wonder how fast that little fifteen horsepower motor will go to compensate for that. He hasn't actually cranked it up."

Bill said that he had been wondering the same thing. "It could take a long time to go back. We haven't used much fuel, though. I've been watching. I think they can open it up and get it moving faster. The only problem would be that small, protected prop. It's not very big."

We discussed it more, and I was somewhat relieved to know that Bill had thought about it too. I put it aside for later. "I think that we will actually be leaving Peru and floating into Bolivia sometime tomorrow, Sir Izaak Walton."

"Do we need any visa or passport stuff, Robin Hood?"

"Who knows? Go to sleep—gotta see Bolivia tomorrow."

Nighttime in a tent without light, TV, radio, or anything but a snore coming from the foot of your lumpy, rock-hard bed gives you time to think about things: how far you've come, how far it is to go back and what there is to be gained by going farther. We have spent days really moving, around numerous wide-sweeping bends too numerous to count, covering a lot of miles, maybe as far as fifty to seventy-five miles in a day. We have enjoyed this strange new habitat, but it was no longer new. There seemed to be the same muddy caiman, herons, butterfly swarms and those nosey jungle pheasants that crash-land overhead. Jose and El Capitan haven't said anything much for days.

The trip back was getting longer every bend we took. I was getting homesick for at least a cold drink and a shower, even for one of Kohler's finest porcelain thrones.

Chapter 10

Phantom Visit in the Night

This night we went to sleep in a forest that seemed denser than usual and with a few more strange noises, some new ones. Giant kapok trees spread their buttressed roots so wide that the circumference can be about thirty feet at the base. Vines draped on the lower canopy level trees. Our tent was about ten feet from the edge of a cliff overlooking a dry creek bed that led to the river below. We were well above the high-water mark of rainy season.

It was after midnight when I woke up with the urge to make a full-service lavatory visit. It was more serious than usual so I grabbed a roll of T-paper, a flashlight and, half awake, started my well-practiced exit through the zippered corner of the mosquito net. On my back, head first, flashlight in my mouth, I started backing out, dragging my legs. Once my head was out of the tent, I reached back with both hands for a good grip on the ground for my final pull out. It was then that my right hand squished into what I imagine feels like sticking your hand in a warm dish of quiche Lorraine, without the dish. I knew what it was. It was a big turd—a fresh, warm, animal feces pie with a liquid topping.

There wasn't the tiniest doubt about it. The smell was just beginning to hit me. I screamed silently to myself, dropping the flashlight from my mouth, trying not to wake the jungle, holding my shit-loaded hand paralyzed in the air, and being careful not to touch anything.

Some sizeable animal not only had the cojones to come around our tent, but decided to leave us a special personal gift in the worst place. It was still warm. What kind of animal donated this mess? Right next to our tent? Deer usually poop pellets, as do rodents. This one was a fresh pile, like a cow pie. We had a bold visitor, a big one.

At that moment I didn't care what had left this gift or where it was now. My hand was full of shit.

The smell was a blast of some noxious mixture of ammonia and vomit. I couldn't touch anything with my hand. There was no question about what to do. I was headed down to the river to wash it off. Sliding to the river in bare feet and jockey shorts was ugly; I was plowing through underbrush, stickers and rocks. I stuck my hand in the river water and used the mud to help clean it off. Only briefly it crossed my mind that piranha might be awakened by the swishing around, but at that moment I didn't care.

Climbing up the bank was worse than the slide down. I was hot and sweaty again. It was the middle of the night. I thought most animals were asleep. Not this nocturnal phantom pooper... and the mosquitoes. I just hoped it wasn't some angry thing with claws and teeth that wanted to get into our tent. In my haste, I had left the corner unzipped. I wondered if maybe a green mamba or a cozy pit-viper might have decided to enter and curl up with Bill while I was gone. That's all we needed at this point.

High mud cliffs visible only during the dry season.

I managed to finish my original task, hanging with one arm around a sapling, dropping drawers, and keeping the flashlight in my mouth while looking around for shining eyes in the jungle. I returned to the tent and with a stick pushed as much of the "quiche surprise" as possible over the nearby cliff, followed by launching the stick after it. Those sickening, shiny, green manure flies had not yet discovered this banquet. I was overheated, bruised, scratched, mosquito bitten and frustrated when I slid back into the tent and rezipped it.

The snoring Guillermo hadn't moved. I tried to get back to sleep, but that putrid, eye-watering odor still clung to my nose. What species of creature was so willing to share even his most personal waste materials with perfect strangers remains unknown to this day. One thing for sure, I would not be biting any fingernails on my right hand for at least a year.

No chickens to wake us next morning meant that our batman, Jose, woke us. He had some coffee ready. I could hardly wait to ruin my fellow travelers' breakfast with my tale of the "late night phantom shitter," which I did, but wasn't sure they believed me. I wished I had saved them a sample. Even if our guides did believe me, they didn't seem to care.

Bill yawned and mumbled, "You grew up on a farm, didn't you? So...? What's the big deal, farmer boy?" as he bit off a chunk of hard bread.

We had other, more important, things to worry about. We were running low on Brazil nuts, the powdered sugar ones.

I went back to looking at my only map. It was a map of Peru that included parts of adjacent countries, but not much detail. Since we were on the Madre de Dios River, I tried to estimate where we would go if we lost power on our little pecke-pecke engine and were at the mercy of the river current only. It appeared that there was no city or town on the river with its name in bold enough print size to be considered even as large as Puerto Maldonado. It seemed to be about 500 miles downstream to Porto Velho, Brazil, which on the map looked like a city, but that was also questionable. It was deep into the Amazon valley. Anyway, there was no way we would make it drifting for 500 miles.

I asked Victor what we would do if the motor went bad and got the answers I expected. First, he said that it was a new engine and "No problemas." I hoped he wasn't going to tell me it was under warranty. He didn't. Second, he said he would fix it. I was sure he didn't have parts and very few tools. He said he was good with motors. No third remedy. Just as we had thought, if it broke down we were S.O.L. until word of us reached civilization or we could be passed upriver by some other vessel. What other vessel? Since we left, we hadn't seen anything bigger than a piece of carved out log floating and an Indian with a wet ass squatting in it.

I worked on constructing some sentences in Spanish so that I could have a good and serious discussion with Victor on his plans for this trip and his experience overall. Something told me he had taken us very far from his normal haunts. Besides, he couldn't even tell me what kind of beast treated us to that charitable, tent-side turd last night. He was only sure that it was not a snake or a chicken. Thanks, Captain. Farm boys know at least that.

As we left that morning, I continued to be concerned that we were going very far downstream, maybe a couple hundred miles or more from Puerto Maldonado. By late morning, I calculated that we were out of Peru and well into Bolivia. I'd seen no signs, of course, just counted the river bends.

Chapter 11

A Native Village

That afternoon we stopped early at a muddy landing where a couple of dugout canoes were parked. It was at the foot of a steep cliff. A path zigzagged up the face of it. Jose told us to climb it. Reaching the top was a chore but, arriving there, we saw some natives. They looked like they were in a permanent residence with a few small shacks, a woman on a loom and a permanent hooded fireplace with something cooking. Some kind of animal was roasting with legs splayed out and head missing. It looked like a skinny pig but, skinless and decapitated, we couldn't tell what kind of animal it was. We weren't invited to dinner anyway, so who cares.

I couldn't help wondering if they also boiled their water.

Bill and I became the captain's weird foreign exhibits, sort of the visiting celebrities or the stupid gringos, we weren't sure which. We were taller, dressed differently than any of them, our hair and skin coloring different, and we didn't speak their language. Other than that, we fit in perfectly. When we talked to ourselves we were usually laughing at something, and of course, they had no idea what we had found so funny or what we said. We didn't know if any of these people had ever visited a city, seen a movie or encountered anything electrical. There were no cities, towns or even airplane contrails overhead. Without roads, they probably never saw motor vehicles. There is something uncomfortable and helpless about meeting someone so completely different and aboriginal.

We gave them some of our trove of ballpoint pens from Walmart. They loved them, but I wasn't sure they could use them. I didn't see anything that looked like paper. They didn't do the most usual thing one does with a new writing instrument—try it. They just looked it over.

One little boy had a pet monkey clutching him as if he was growing there. It was cute but I couldn't help thinking about whether a monkey of some kind could have been the midnight phantom pooper. It didn't really seem like the time to ask them what kind of turds and bathroom habits these little monkeys had. Besides, this one was too little and clung to the kid as though his life depended on it.

I looked at my hand again to make sure there wasn't anything left, even under the fingernails.

Our new Indian friends were pointing to a young man, small in stature but well-muscled. He had two teeth that we could see, carried a long oar, and was drawing much attention from the people in this village. Jose introduced him to us as a complete hombre de la selva "jungle man" who lived all the time by himself in the jungle. He was a small Tarzan, maybe a foot shorter than Johnny Weismueller but just as well dressed. His entire worldly possessions sat in those two dugout canoes near where we parked our pecke-pecke boat.

The jungle man seemed well organized. His boats contained homemade rope; four short, hand-carved paddles; a wooden platform for grinding or cutting; and a machete that made Bill

Another native with his canoe, hewn from single tree trunk. Also shows mud in tiers as river level drops in dry season.

green with envy. A large wicker basket brimmed with pots, and their lids sat next to a basket full of cassava, the Indians' favorite starch. He had blankets and a waterproof cover, which he probably used to keep the rain off of him, since he didn't appear to have a tent. A bow, strung and ready, and four long arrows were within easy reach from his seat in the rear. Both canoes were carved from tree trunks but with a higher quality carving than most we had seen. They were smooth and a little deeper than most.

None of the dugouts used in this area are deep enough to stay dry. They are more like concave slices of large trees that float on top of the water but have some water flowing over and usually have a puddle of water in them. There are no seats; the Indians just sit cross-legged and paddle from a position back of center so that the bow is up and can go over some waves.

The jungle boy was treated like an admired celebrity. People crowded around to chat with him. We could not find out any more about him other than he was a loner, living on the move. He was welcomed to the village and fed when he came. He may have brought fish or game with him to contribute to the camp, but we could not tell.

The woman on the loom never stopped weaving, even for a curious peek at us, or at the jungle man. We guessed that she wasn't in the textile workers union. She didn't even take breaks. It was amazing to me, having worked around textile mills in South Carolina, to see weaving with the shuttle being thrown through by this woman instead of the machine gun speed of today's automatic looms. She must have needed months to make a yard or two of cloth.

At El Capitan Yarikawa's signal, we slid back down the cliff to our boat, took a picture and another look at jungle man's canoes, then were on our way downstream. The jungle on both sides looked just as it had for many miles and days. Brazil nut trees were immense stand-alone features, sprouting limbs only above the canopy. Kapok trees were very much the same, but with red leaves or blooms this time of year. We were going to make camp in Bolivia that night.

The travel down this latte-colored waterway had a beauty all its own. There were only two basic colors. The heavy shades of green vegetation came right to the edge of the smooth, tan liquid. The wide parts of the river sometimes spread very wide, perhaps a half mile. It was calm. Not much of a breeze could make it past the forest. It was a calm lake, except that it was moving. From shore you were reminded of the flow by a floating leaf or a ripple of current beside our parked gondola.

While we unloaded, Jose was fishing. He put meat on the hook, smacked the water a few times and dinner came. Bill also did some fishing and caught a small piranha. Actually, it was very small. I insisted on taking his picture holding it in case it was an I.G.F.A. (International Game Fish Association) world record. "Smallest red bellied piranha caught on rod and reel, 10-lb. test leader (footnote: Madre de Dios Region, Peru, 1990)."

Might make the fall issue if we returned home in time.

Dinner consisted of fresh piranha, (not Bill's trophy fish) rice, banana hockey pucks and muddy water coffee, topped off with some stale bread slathered with peanut butter for dessert. Who could ask for more?

One of the creatures Jose caught was a stingray. He cut off the poisonous spline, wrapped it in a piece of cloth and put it into his bag. He left the rest of the ray in the boat. After it had bled all over the boat, he finally threw it overboard. I asked him why he saved the spline, and he replied that he was going to make some medicine. Asked and answered, I guess. I had already learned that follow-up questions led only to deeper confusion. Maybe at some later time he could tell us. Right then we were hungry.

The pall of uncertainty over our growing distance from civilization, and the time it might take to return, was beginning to overshadow my interest in what would be new and exciting around the next bend of the river. The trees and vines under the canopy had been the same for days. The river remained muddy.

I didn't say much to Bill at this point, but I was wondering if my partner was actually oblivious to the inherent dangers of our growing reach. He must have had some concern, but it didn't show. Of course, nothing was going to stop our laughs, but it was taking up more of my thoughts every day. Our guides and traveling companions seemed not to share my concern. They were only "out of town," so to speak. We were a lot more than that. It was clear that I was the designated worrier on this trip. Guillermo seemed to be clearly having an insouciant safari. At least it seemed so.

I kept thinking of my philosophical hero, Yogi Berra, who once said, "If you don't know where you're going, you might end up someplace else." That made just as much sense to me as any information we had received so far from our captain and crew. In Florida I could take my boat and travel due south from Naples and reach the outer marker of Key West and its northwest channel in about four hours at a rate of about 24 knots. That's a little over 100 miles. I knew it took trawler type boats about twice as long and they travel about as fast as we were going down stream. Roughly estimating our total time so far, our distance had to be well over 200 miles of river travel from Puerto Maldonado. We had seen a lot of jungle.

I finally had a talk with our little captain, asked him some questions, and then reported to Bill. "Guillermo, I just talked to the admiral to see what his plans were and what we could expect and what he knew about this trip and how much experience Victor and Jose had with this kind of trip. I put together this question: 'Victor, Qual es el viaje mas largo que ha tomado?' I worked on it a long time so he would understand what I was saying. I was asking him what was the longest trip they had ever taken on this river. I wanted to see what he knew about this trip ahead that he was planning for us. Guess what he said?"

"Pecke-pecke" boat carrying two gringos, Captain Victor,
crewman Jose, and all supplies for this adventure.

"I can't. What?"

"He said, 'Este.' That means this one.... This is the longest trip he has ever taken. He doesn't even know the area we are in now. How do you like that?"

Bill just stared at me for a minute, trying to let it sink in.

I broke the silence, "Isn't that a confidence builder?"

"That Hunyak!" Bill said as he drew a big breath and spat his spent wad of Redman's finest chewing tobacco into the rain forest. With the most disgusted look Bill could make, he added, "He doesn't know his own ass. Jose's worse."

"It makes you think twice about these guys. Capitan Yarikawa very much wants to show us the pampas. It is supposed to be something special to see. I can't imagine..."

"Pampas?" Bill interrupted, "Pampas is like Wyoming or Illinois—just a prairie—isn't it? Why would we want to see that? We came here to see the jungle, didn't we?

"Maybe because he has never seen it himself...you think? Or he thinks it's something special. We live in the damned pampas? If you think about it, these guys may never have been there before. They grew up and spent their entire lives in this jungle, as far as we know. That's all they know. Oh, except for the, ha, inner-city life in Puerto Maldonado."

"Wonder if that means that Barbara Fearis has never been this far either. No wonder she never charged us anything. She just gave us that huge advice sheet, a couple of names, made everything sound like a validated excursion on board a cruising vessel with two experienced native guides. We were the big hunyaks, whatever that means. She is now the P.T. Barnum of obscure jungle trips."

"The pampas must be only lore to Admiral Victor and his crew. Something they've only heard about. They are taking advantage of this trip to see something new. Just think, open land, fields of grass, clusters of small trees. Maybe he expects cowboys, vaqueros, caballeros, or cattle rustlers. He may never have seen a cow or a horse, as far as we know. That would naturally be a curiosity for him, just like the jungle is for us. Well, there aren't cowboys and cattle in this part of the world, but I have read that the birds and animals are different than in the jungle."

"Another problem we might think about is that we would have to leave this river and steam our way upstream on Rio Heath to get there. That is another tributary that comes down from the Andes and one that our captain has never seen. He might not know the current there. What if he uses up all our fuel? I didn't see any service stations on the way, did you?"

We shared another big laughing session, which probably made them curious. The language barrier made it impossible to share jokes with them.

We had finally come to terms with the fact that our two leaders were not geniuses. The confidence we had in them at the start—with their adroit stream navigation, boatmanship and efficiency in setting up our camp—had been seriously eroded by Jose's bat beating, their inability to give us answers and this latest zeal to see some damn prairie. We knew we weren't that safe, so it was time to start erring on the safe side. Already we were probably too far, in time, to keep us from dying from appendicitis or some unexpected infection or injury. How many days even from a telephone? Or penicillin? Or a defibrillator? We decided to limit debate on the motion to turn around and head for home to about ten seconds. There being no further discussion, we took a vote of those present. The vote was tallied: two in favor, zero opposed. We would make a U-turn, skip the pampas tour and head back to Puerto Maldonado.

We further agreed to advise our fearless leader that evening that we had seen the American pampas all of our lives and we hate it. We came here to the selva in the first place to get out of a pampas. We wanted to go back through the selva, see things we missed, and return to beautiful downtown Puerto Maldonado.

It would be an even longer trip since we would be fighting a current upstream not gliding downstream.

We guessed that we were in Bolivia by now but there was no way of knowing. There was no such thing as any border indications in a jungle, no customs or immigration. If so, we're probably here illegally. Illegal aliens. If we actually were in Bolivia, neither the Peruvian government nor the Bolivian government knew about it. And for that matter, neither did the U.S. government. If we disappear now, we will probably show up in 100 years in some archeologist's bag, marked, "Unidentifiable bones, DNA tests show to be non-native ancestry."

Chapter 12

Bolivia Boss – The Fearsome El Jefe

We pulled up to the foot of a wooded hill that had a wooden planked dock. A strange sight in the jungle. From the dock there was a path leading up the hill. It wasn't a pit stop. The crew, Jose, unloaded our stuff.

It appeared that we were stopping where we did because we were in Bolivia and required to pay homage to either a real or self-appointed chief or toll collector. We never knew which, but Victor made it clear that he was handling this himself and we should sit still. We were going to camp in the wooded area not far from the top of a hill where we could see this chief's cabins at the very top.

After hauling our bags, tents and provisions, but before setting up camp, Victor took us up to the cabin where we met "El Jefe," the chief of this place, Porto Heath, an area near the confluence of the Heath and the Madre de Dios Rivers in Bolivia. We never heard his real name.

El Jefe was a larger-than-life character with a big toothy grin, proudly showing one gold tooth in the top row of pearly whites. That happy grin could turn into a stormy scowl at an instant, to make a point. His face was a moonscape with craters left from acne—more likely from some kind of pox—and he looked like he combed his thick black and gray hair with a greasy mechanic's rag. He sat at a table with his only light, a fat, white candle sitting on it, with only its drippings to hold it in place. His desk was bare wood, with the finish of a workbench.

In a strange, startling move, El Jefe suddenly stabbed a hunting knife into the wooden table and left it there. Maybe it was a little punctuation he felt was necessary to emphasize his authority and toughness. If it was to get our attention, it worked. A silent period followed, while we considered what he had just done. It wasn't actually a Chamber of Commerce key to the city. At least we knew one thing about him: He didn't have high regard for his furniture.

We were never able to determine whether he claimed to be a Bolivian official checking us entering the country or a Peruvian official checking us leaving Peru. All we knew was that we needed our passports, there were some negotiations, some undisclosed amount of money changed hands from Victor to El Jefe and we were invited to take a seat at a wooden bench against the cabin wall while El Jefe pretended to read our passports. He had no questions.

We knew that the toll or gratuity wasn't much, or wasn't "official," because Victor didn't ask us for any money. I think he paid it from the change he never gave us from the grocery money and/or he didn't want to have us asking any questions about any payments of any kind. This entire visit seemed rather unofficial, but we were not about to argue the matter.

Mounted on the wall above the chief's head was a rifle. A small basket containing some papers sat on one side of the desk. Jefe was loud, pausing for approval after every pronouncement he would make, like, "Comprendo?" Or "Verdad?" Or "Si?" Or "huh?" After I explained that I knew only a little Spanish, he was happy to regale us with his even smaller vocabulary of English. "We friends, yes?" was his favorite expression.

A couple of his men apparently hung around there only to see to his wishes, and he had them bring a beer, just one big one. It was then that Victor asked me to give El Jefe 10,000 Intis for a bottle of beer. ($26 at that time.) Another "tribute to the big boss."

After that little transaction, Victor and Jose left this joyous reception to set up our camp while we were left with the local Jefe to drink toasts to our friendship. El Jefe was truly a blustering bully and a slob. He was loud, obnoxious and insisted on teaching us the way the natives drink, refill, drink more, pledge their friendship and drink some more.

He explained that passing around this quart bottle of beer was a tradition, one of friendship. I felt a little conspicuous when I wiped off the bottle each time it came to me, but I did it anyway. Bill didn't drink, but he tipped it up as if he did. The beer was said to be cooled in the river, but it was not really cool. It left a bitter aftertaste like some old, wet cardboard. He kept passing it, first to Bill, then to me, then to his first subordinate, then the second one and back to him. It went on, with his drinking, talking, bragging about his importance and his power. As he gulped more on each pass, we gulped less, until his "To us friendship" had deteriorated to just "tus flendshit."

He explained several times how he was the Jefe of the whole area around here, using both arms in a wide—spreading gesture. "Todos, as far as we could see, Rio Madre de Dios, Rio Heath, all of people, all over. I am El Jefe, all over here." He waved his hand.

There was absolutely nothing to see but trees. If we had known the Bolivian National Anthem, we would have been obliged to jump up and, at full attention, sing it, on the spot, a capella.

I asked El Jefe where he learned the English and he said something so incoherent I decided not to try to unravel it and just said, "Oh, bueno," and let it go.

Bill was having a small side problem of his own. One of El Jefe's men had an eye on Bill's combat boots. Bill had gone to an army surplus store before we left and bought some of the hot weather, mesh top combat boots, the kind they wore in Viet Nam. El Jefe's "number two" guy made his desire known. He kept looking at Bill, then his boots, then smiling, then holding his foot up next to Bill's, looking at him, smiling. He hadn't yet offered anything to trade for them. Watching Bill as he tried to ignore him, I found very entertaining. It was all I could do to keep from saying, "Hey, Guillermo, why don't you let your friend try them on?"

He then began to look at Bill's big knife, also a jungle survival type that I am sure they had never seen. He wanted to feel it too. Bill was getting the message but didn't like it. He wasn't about to fork over his shoes or his knife. Watching him try to ignore this big admirer was worth the price of admission.

Just then, and perfect timing for Bill, out of the hush of the surrounding jungle, we heard the low rumbling of a diesel engine down at the river; it was the kind of pounding that you can almost feel before you hear it. The river was about a hundred yards down the hill from us. At first, I paid no special attention to it. El Jefe's man went from admiring Bill's footwear to a shocking dash out and down to meet the boat. It was a small scow carrying cargo. It appeared to be about thirty feet long and ten feet wide. It edged over to the small dock and tied up. It was after sunset but not yet dark, and we could see a man come out of the boat to talk to El Jefe's man. They exchanged loud words and the man then returned to the boat and restarted it.

El Jefe's man rushed up the hill to the cabin. Clearly out of breath and unhappy, he reported things to El Jefe, while the boat started pounding upstream again. Suddenly El Jefe's friendly grin turned dark and menacing. His eyebrows slanted and dropped, his mouth tightened, and he jumped up, reached for his rifle on the wall. He bounded outside and fired six shots in the direction of the boat.

Bill and I stared at each other. It was becoming hard to see outside. After the shots, the diesel engine immediately slowed down to idling speed. The barge was drifting backward in the current toward the dock again. Bill looked out and saw that the barge had a tarp covering something near the bow. He hoped it was not a mounted machine gun. Was this going to be a war? We just sat there with no idea what would happen next.

The boat pulled into El Jefe's small dock again, tied up and stopped the engine. In a few minutes we saw a man leave the boat and climb uphill to the cabin. El Jefe went out of the cabin to meet him coldly, with no words spoken, no handshake, only some polite mumbles. They were coming together toward El Jefe's cabin. As they passed close by on the way, I distinctly heard the boat's pilot say "Yo pagare, pero...," (that clearly meant, "I will pay, but..." then some jabbering.) We guessed that those few gunshots had added real emphasis to El Jefe's request for a toll, sent via his lieutenant. Apparently, the scow captain told Jefe's man to go scratch, but when some bullets started to splash off his bow or hit his vessel, he saw fit to revisit his earlier decision.

Things calmed down. The man returned to the barge, went on his way upstream, and El Jefe returned to our company, leaning his rifle proudly against the table—another symbol of his power and bravado. We were no more comfortable than before his attack. He obviously had decided it was not necessary to explain to us any of this evening's activities, so we continued to drain the beer. When we finally had our last few toasts, we thought we could take leave from his grace to return to our camp. We quietly and politely did so, leaving the almighty Jefe to his beer, his hangover and his rifle reloading.

Later, Jose and Victor told us that the boat contained contraband and that it always costs more if the cargo is illegal. Huh! The nerve of those guys to think bribing, protection, or any kind of corruption was the same price, regardless of the cargo. Victor had no idea what the cargo was or where it was going. Or if he did, he wasn't saying. The lack of any paperwork of any kind made this transaction, like our visit, appear a bit unofficial. Nothing about any part of El Jefe's operation appeared to be official.

"Billy, you ought to be glad that boat came along. You were about to lose your new boots to the Vice Jefe there, weren't you? I got a big kick out of watching you trying to ignore him, ha. Maybe you should have offered them to him as a goodwill gesture. He's your new friend, you unfriendly gringo."

"Boots?" he growled back at me, "he wanted my knife too. Didn't you see him pointing at it, touching it and asking to see it? I even took it out and let him touch it but I wouldn't hand it to him. I had to shake my head no. That's while you and the Jefe were saluting each other and choking down that rot gut, imitation beer. He was a real pain-in-the-ass."

"Bill, let me tell you something. You're real lucky."

"Why, what do you mean?"

"We are in the deep, dark jungle and ran into a guy who can take a gun off the wall, fire it six times at a moving boat, make it stop and tie up, then have the captain run up a hill to pay homage and money to him. You do realize that if El Jefe, the shooter, looked at you and said, 'Hey der, Beeg Boy, geeve my assistant your boots and dat knife,' it's likely that you would finish this trip barefoot and unarmed."

Bill looked at me, thoughtfully blank, and said, "Hmm, I guess you're right. Maybe we'd better get out of here before he thinks about that."

Chef Jose had finished setting up tents and was well into his dishwashing practice. Jose always washed the previous day's dishes in the afternoon before eating the evening meal, although this was a little later than usual. I never found out whether that had something to do with some custom peculiar to the Southern hemisphere, his upbringing, or just Jose.

Washing before eating might have made sense. We weren't sure. He never used soap, just muddy water and lots of rubbing, with bare hands. We figured that the mud acted like an abrasive and helped the dishes almost sparkle—almost. At least any dirt or bugs collected during the day were rubbed off before dinner.

All waste material was tossed in the river: food, bones, wrappers, and anything else. One time, Bill had inquired about some plastic we had seen caught in driftwood sticks in the stream. It was blue film and we had seen it before—so completely unusual in this pristine environment. Bill asked about what happens to that trash. The answer from Jose was something like "Los animales comen." The animals eat it? Blue plastic? Another statement that wasn't worth pursuing, but I did anyway.

"Los comen, animales?" making an eating gesture.

"Si," Jose replied. Well, there was no use going on with that questioning. He said it as if he really believed that animals ate the plastic. It made for some handy explanations of almost all other jungle mysteries after that, though. Any question that would come up later, one of us usually solved it with, "Oh, no problema; the animals will eat it."

Where was Barbara Fearis when we needed her?

Actually, it was about that time on the trip that Jose and Victor let slip that their nickname for Barbara Fearis was "Tootsie." Surely, they were talking about the Dustin Hoffman movie, where an actor dressed himself up as a woman to get some job at a hospital. I guess they thought they knew us and our sense of humor well enough for us to enjoy it. We didn't know that there was even a movie house in Puerto Maldonado where they could have seen it. They told us that Tootsie came to Puerto Maldonado for long periods of time, sat on her one-person pecke pecke under a shade canopy, and just wrote or wandered around. That's all we could find out. We all had a good chuckle and a shrug of the shoulders that says to everyone, "Quien sabe?" (Who knows?)

Our meal was truly boring. Something to fill the void, only. Even though it was our first bountiful Bolivian banquet, one might have noticed it was similar to many others we had consumed in Peru. Bill was starting to look like a fried banana, and I was probably starting to smell like a dead piranha. We were still inspecting our rice carefully on each mouthful. Our hair itched. Our clothes were stiffening. We slept, but it was off and on. We were often tired, maybe from riding in that canoe and always sticky from sweat. We religiously took our malaria pills and Pepto Bismol.

For the first few days of the trip we had seen new things. Now, every day and every mile we observed the same kapok and Brazil nut trees poking through the canopy like towers, the puddles on the sides of every stream had thousands of butterflies in all colors, and the herons would fly over when we scared them up from their quiet shoreline, shallow water stalking places. It was starting to look the same every day.

It was enough and we were ready to go.

I had photographed most of the wonders here. Perhaps, the trip back to Puerto Maldonado could provide some interesting things we hadn't already seen. The risk of being so far away and so isolated from every means of travel and contact from everything was no longer worth extending our journey. When the river was wide, we got no protection from that scorching sun, and there were many hours left to roast before relief.

Over dinner I explained to Captain Yarikawa and crew, Jose, as clearly as I could, our decision to turn around the next day and make our way back to Puerto Maldonado. Victor shook his head and explained that the pampas was really only one (long) day up the Rio Heath and then we would return. That meant adding at least two more days plus one in the pampas, then the return home. I disagreed. We gave all our reasons, which, of course, were meaningless to Victor. I insisted. "No, Victor, mañana, vamos a regresar a Puerto Maldonado. Vamos a Puerto Maldonado, ahora."

He nodded his head in a rather reluctant agreement, a little disappointed maybe, but we were the customers and that's what we wanted. Everything seemed clear. I actually thought he would be happy to hear it. After all, he gets the same money—shorter trip, less spent, more profit, but he seemed ambivalent. I didn't really understand.

After dinner I did a little recalculating about our return trip upriver. It was dark and I didn't want to use much battery power, but I could quickly see that certain routes around islands would save us time. Some jungle visits we took on the way could be omitted on the return trip, and we could gain fifty miles or more bypassing Lake Valencia and the Huarayo Indian fishing camp. As much as we would hate to miss a good big whiff of their community latrine, some sacrifices were necessary for the sake of speed. Anyway, we figured that if you've had one good whiff, the memory would probably remain vivid for a lifetime.

"Hey, Guillermo, let's hope for no more uninvited visitors tonight unless they're potty trained, and positively no noisy jungle chickens in the morning."

Bill and I went to sleep that night feeling a little more relaxed about everything and what lay ahead. We knew we were going to a destination, not some mystery even farther out of touch than we already were. Our risks were going to be fewer, not greater. We planned to look for more animals, take more pictures and check some interesting areas we had floated past on previous days.

Chapter 13

Decision—U-Turn

The next morning, we arose later than usual. Amazing how life without alarm chickens plus a good plan for the day can change things. The sun had already shown its light through the clouds in the eastern horizon. The sky above us was a beautiful ceiling of billowing dark purple clouds with some pale blue sky showing through some of the fluffy openings. Below the ceiling was a fire-red horizon, slashed horizontally with the blinding white streaks of the sun's fire. It was a massive palate of sky hues, a panorama of changing color that nearly surrounded us. Our camp was high on the hill, just high enough to see this sky sitting on top of an irregular, dark green jungle canopy, below which was the wide river, solid red from the reflection.

It was a spectacular sight. I had to take several photos of it.

Victor and Jose took their time this morning because they thought it necessary to wait and say a proper farewell to El Jefe with whatever they considered jungle protocol required. Jefe's hangover probably whispered to him this morning to stay in the sack for a couple of extra hours.

When his rustic majesty finally made his disheveled, droopy-eyed appearance, we all thanked him profusely for his hospitality. His night's sleep had not made him prettier. Bill and I, performing with our most serious, straight-faced insincerity, told him that we would welcome him to the United States someday if he ever visited. We added that we hoped he would visit soon. We had left no name or address and he hadn't kept a record of the passports, so we were safe.

Heading for our boat, we waved goodbye to El Jefe, the jungle boss, as if we were really going to miss him. It was fortunate that our noses didn't grow like Pinocchio's. Best of all, Bill escaped with his combat boots on his feet rather than on his Bolivian admirer, and his trusty survival knife strapped on and ready to be used.

After we seated ourselves on our familiar plank in the boat, a quick look at our provisions in the bow compartment left us wondering what we would have done if we had extended this trip farther. Even more urgently, what were we going to use on this return trip? We were about out of supplies already. Judging by miles traveled and our speed, the return trip ahead of us was destined to be at least as long as coming to this point downstream.

"We may have to do some serious fishing," Bill volunteered. He then turned his attention to Jose, "Hey, Peckahead, where-o are-o el rest of the Brazil nuts?" he shouted at him while he pushed off the bow.

At this moment, Bill was no different than any of us Americans. We think that if we speak English loudly enough and slowly enough, any foreigner will understand.

(Note: By now, we had renamed Jose, "Peckahead," partly because he deserved it with his bonehead bat-beating episode, his knucklehead behavior generally, and because he occupied the head of our pecke-pecke boat. We considered his new name not only descriptive but technically and politically correct.)

It was as if the handsome Peckahead Jose never intended to come forth with our last bag of Brazil nuts, but when he finally did, we understood his reluctance. These nuts were caked with brown sugar. Casi Cielo, Almost heaven. They were unbelievably toe-tappin' delicious enough to make anyone hum. They were absolutely the best yet.

Was he hoping we wouldn't ask? Was he hoping we would die of rabid bat bites or poisonous water so he would not have to share? They were worth the wait. He grabbed and jammed some in his mouth first, so it could not have been another of his botched homicide attempts. After all, "Good enough to die for" is only a figure of speech. We all went into an uncontrollable Brazil nut feeding frenzy.

Native village houses, with bicycles and wheelbarrows for transport.

In this wide, mahogany-colored expanse of the river, Victor swung the boat in a large circle and headed upstream for the first time, navigating around one of the big islands in what appeared to be a different channel than we had used before. A mile or so up, this side of the island revealed a large, shallow wading pond of several acres—full of roseate spoonbills. We sat transfixed as they waded, sweeping their heads back and forth in the water for whatever small fish, snails or other morsels they could grab.

They sported a spectacular shade of pink and red that rarely appears in nature. It may be similar in color to the flamingo but just a little brighter, more like desert pink. The color is so appealing that it just forces anyone to watch the birds, especially the undersides of their wings when they fly.

With this new supply of Brazil nuts within arm's reach, it was all I could do with two hands to get my share of nuts, grab the camera and snap a couple of pictures of these spoonbills. With them were some wading herons with necks and legs so skinny that it is amazing they were strong enough to walk and be able to swallow anything. A new sound came out of the forest too. A bird made a Pee-whoop sound and lots of them. Pee-whoop, pee-whoop. Never saw the bird making the noise, but it was loud.

A couple of large iguanas looked up at us with their 360-degree turret-like eyes, then scurried into hiding. They reminded us of little Godzillas, those jerky Japanese movie monsters from the deep. Their appearance of armor plate alone should be enough to scare off a predator.

Maybe our rerouting for the return would bring us more things to see and photograph. I still hoped to see a jaguar and an anaconda.

Bill and I felt a clear sense of relief in the fact that we were returning rather than continuing into this unknown world for an unknown period of time. A couple of other details offered us encouragement at the start of this return trip. First and most importantly, the pecke-pecke motor could be run much faster than we had thought, judging from the way they ran it downstream. We could make a little more speed against the current than I expected, not nearly as fast as downstream, but still, decent progress. Surprisingly, this small motor, even with its tiny propeller, was capable of about eleven or twelve knots, or about fourteen mph with no current, or about seven to nine mph against the current going upstream. Even with all things working, however, including the weather and barring surprises, we had a good four to five full days of travel to reach Puerto Maldonado.

Secondly, Captain Yarikawa seemed to be very good at picking the best routes to go upstream. He used shortcuts in curves and river bends when going around islands. He did seem to know how to negotiate the river. He knew where to go and where to stop. He knew where the current was slowest, in the eddies and inside the bends. He also guessed well at the shortest route around the many islands. Considering all the bends, I found no way, at least on my map, to measure the distance we had come on this trip. It was more than 200 miles of river travel. We would have to run longer hours during the day, with fewer stops, keeping all fingers crossed for the health of this little motor.

Neither Bill nor I had ever dared to question whether they had enough fuel in those two barrels. We couldn't tell anyway, and it would only have been one more thing to worry about.

During one short rest stop, we watched our curious jungle pheasants (hoatzins) awkwardly crashing into some overhead limbs. Now I was certain that they were following us. Why had they landed here? Near a boat? Near people? We couldn't tell if they were the same ones or new ones. They seemed to keep at least one of their group with its bright red eye watching us at all times. They never came real close and tried not to show more than their heads. It was a cinch that they were not gun shy and not afraid of humans. Even pointing them out to Victor and Jose, I couldn't get any more information than Jose holding his nose again, as if the birds smelled bad. With each visit from these curious, crash-landing tree crawlers, my curiosity grew.

Later that day we passed an Indian woman, waist deep in the river, next to a mud bank, washing her clothes. With her, sitting on the mud, was her little boy—naked. How they ever get the clothes clean is a mystery. Once she had wrung out as much of the muddy water as possible, she put them in a pot to carry home. Her presence, alone in this river, meant that we must be near some Indian village we hadn't known existed when we came this way the day before.

Soon after that, we docked and Victor led us up a hill to a flat plateau area where we encountered a native village. It consisted of ten heavily thatched, gable-roofed cabins on stilts, which kept them four feet off the ground. The roofs were thick, with long eaves down over the sides. The ends were open but each had a small eaves over it for protection. It was obvious that they were built to resist heavy rains when the season arrived. Numerous short, dark-skinned natives seemed curious about us visitors. An old woman sat on the ground with a big homemade mortar and pestle, grinding grain and then repeatedly dumping it from one elevated bowl to a lower one, letting the lighter chaff blow away in the breeze.

Their clothing looked homemade but not like some tribes that were known to make appearances along the Madre de Dios over the years that just wore a frontal black loincloth or nothing.

People crowded around to see us. Inbreeding in this tribe was obvious. As far as I could tell, they could all have been part of the same family: same builds, same black bushy hair, facial features and coloring. Victor talked to them and his gestures seemed to indicate that he was explaining us and asking permission to move about the village. He was getting nods that seemed to be agreement. He led us through this nameless village, showing us some of their activities—wood working, weaving, cooking—all the while explaining to the villagers who we were.

He was not speaking Spanish. He was using the same language he used with the fishermen. I heard a few Spanish-sounding words, but the tone was more guttural. The Indian tribesmen were not a very demonstrative lot, but they were curious. There was little conversation among them as we went by their shacks, which had openings at both ends but no doors.

In one shack Jose was pleased to point out a party of about six women breast-feeding their young papooses (papeese). All were sitting quietly, tending to the task, with typical indifference to us. We didn't know whether they considered it a social affair, but they were all together, not chatting, sipping cocktails or snacking. There was very little talking, and we seemed to be invisible.

I can report that Huarayo mothers overwhelmingly prefer the left breast for feeding, unless, of course, there was another group holding a right-breasted get together in another cabin not on our tour. Maybe it was just left-breast day—or something. We wondered but we didn't ask. We already felt a little awkward as it was, neither of us having read Emily Post's rules for men at Huarayo Indian left-breast feeding fetes. We just moved on.

One of the cabins was a classroom. In it were some strange desks, bench seats and a green board with chalk. About ten children of all sizes and both genders were assembled. They invited us in to show us something in the classroom. They all appeared nervous and shy. We thought they were going to grab some chalk and write some Spanish words or something. There was not a chance of that.

They weren't going to show us any Spanish academic achievements. Just the opposite. They were Huarayo and proud ones. They began some tribal dance, singing and adding some hand gestures. The choreography could have used a little improvement as it was all very stiff and unrehearsed. They were not good, but we applauded anyway.

Selfishly, I had this thought that I had hauled all those ballpoint pens from Walmart in Naples, Florida, just to help them with their schoolwork, and they showed us a second-rate Indian dance. We also gave them some hard candy.

What was I thinking? None took a pen and curiously started writing on anything which would have been expected. There wasn't even any paper in sight.

They were all very friendly and very grateful for anything. It wasn't long before my selfish feeling turned to total shame. They gave us a handmade Inca type flat straw sombrero, a bow and three arrows for each of us. They seemed to be taken from their own supplies, not some stash of souvenirs ready for visitors. We guessed that they may have had few, if any, visitors at this village so far from everything. Everything was from their jungle resources and traditional tribal art.

These arrows were not toys or tourists' gifts. They were the real working models, ready for hunting and decorated with care. They were over four feet long, made from straight, smooth reeds about one half inch in diameter and fixed with arrowheads fifteen inches long, carved of that iron-hard wood we had seen before. The tips were sharp. Each arrowhead boasted seven barbs carved into it and was fastened onto the shafts with many strands of orange thread. There were two long guidance feathers near the base, applied in spiral to provide a rotation when shot, and four sets of short, flared, decorative feathers tied along the shaft in tightly wound colored thread.

The bows were not elaborate but strong, made from the same iron-like hard wood as the arrowheads. It took a real effort to draw it back, and a special grip on the string to make sure it didn't slip off the arrow since it had no notched insert for the string. So, for a cheap bag of Walmart ballpoint pens and some candy, we were walking off with many long hours of Indian handicraft, artwork and materials. I wondered if Peter Minuit felt as guilty as we did when he bought Manhattan Island for a handful of beads.

Were these the same Huarayo Indians whose grandparents had fired poisonous arrows at Col. Percy Fawcett and his party in his 1910 expedition? Were there still some that resented intruders? Had they weaned themselves of the habit of eating human flesh as part of their ceremonies? These long arrows fit the description and this was the Heath River. Well, if they were, we could always point to the great free fishing lesson that my partner had given them days earlier in Lake Valencia.

It began to rain, not heavily at first, but with very big drops that got attention when they hit our heads. The children were excited. They began to look for puddles, wallowing in the mud, making shapes while sitting in the middle of the largest mud puddles they could find. Workers scurried to take cover. The rain seemed to come as a sudden, big surprise, like the ones during summer in Florida. It stopped just as abruptly. The passing cloud had spoken and was on its way. The sun blasted again and the humidity was stifling.

These Indians were well practiced for rain, living much of their time during the rainy season. Rainfall in this forest was over eighty inches per year.

I asked Victor if this was the same tribe that was in the oxbow lake at the fishing camp and he said it was. That's why there were so few men in the village. They would return from their camp when the catch was complete or they were homesick.

From what we had learned from "Tootsie" Fearis and reading about the Huarayos, they may have once been subservient to the Incas, living on the lower slopes of the Andes, settling on the Andes side of the Madre de Dios river. They are hunter-gatherers, only recently doing some subsistence agriculture. Later I learned that they marry at a young age and when they have children, they consider them entirely a product of the father. The mother is just, in their words, a bag. She is considered a mother and a relative but not considered a contributor to the offspring. Dad gets all the credit or the blame for the offspring.

Marriage and divorce are rather simple in the tribe. There may be some minor celebration for marriage and dowry consideration, but mainly the female just moves in with the man. For a divorce, one just leaves the house and lives somewhere else. No divorce attorneys. What a pleasant fantasy. I could imagine the shock awaiting them with their eventual assimilation into the Peruvian, Spanish, Roman Catholic society and legal system.

Polygamy is practiced, but is a privilege of only the elite male, either a chief or a shaman, both of whom received their status from their fathers. The shaman is a kind of witchdoctor, the only one in the enclave qualified in medicines and in connecting the spirits of the dead to the living in their ceremonies. A shaman can interpret the hallucinations they have during the drinking of the ayahuasca brew they cook up for special ceremonies.

Ayahuasca is a jungle vine boiled with various leaves or herbs and consumed as spiritual medicine. Some of the hallucinations are considered to tell the future of lives, or other revelations. It often makes them sick and miserable. Some men's lives have been known to change completely as a result of these ayahuasca ceremonies and the visions of the future they see for themselves. Some die of overdoses. Bill and I just wanted a little taste, maybe just enough to give us a peek into what kind of animals we used to be. We never got the chance.

Chapter 14

The Bad Revelation

After that cultural awakening tour, we returned to the boat, deposited our plank-hardened derrieres on that hardwood "observation" board, and headed upstream again, watching for caiman, tree boas, monkeys or anything else moving in the jungle. Things in thick jungle often screech when they see a person, but they cannot always be seen. When the engine is turned off, there is an undisturbed silence seldom experienced in the populated world. A human actually welcomes a bird or animal noise of some kind.

As I looked up at some of the giant Brazil nut trees, I was fascinated by the one piece of tree trivia that I knew: Brazil was the only country named after a tree. It was named after the Brazil tree, not the other way around. I was going to remind myself of that and win some bets back home. No use betting Bill. He would just spit and tell me to go scratch and wouldn't pay anyway.

I wondered how they ever gathered the nuts. The trees are enormous. The limbs grow out only at the top, which is farther up and farther out than anyone could reach with long poles. You could not shake one of these trees to make nuts fall even if you rammed it with a Sherman tank.

When we went ashore the next time, I began to question Jose about the harvesting technique they used for gathering Brazil nuts. He simply picked up a ball-shaped pod about the size of a softball that was under one of these monster trees. It was heavy and hard as wood. He broke it open with a rock and there they were, a dozen or more nuts neatly imbedded side by side in a circular pattern like orange sections. Apparently, gatherers have to wait until the pods fall before they can harvest. No picking involved.

The streams had looked different that day. The wading lake and the forest trees were the same but not the overall riverbank. Parts of it were steeper than I remembered as we came downstream. The channel seemed smaller, but we assumed that we were going around islands in different channels.

But then, how many times have we driven through a scenic area somewhere and taken the return route and noticed things from this reverse view that we had missed when looking in the other direction?

I did fear that we had not made much progress this day. When we made camp that night I asked Victor about the stop we had made at the village and how much farther it was to Puerto Maldonado. I wanted to explain to him as diplomatically as possible that we did enjoy visiting the Huarayo village, but we wanted to make a straight trip toward home as an express, not a sightseeing cruise, and with only minimum stops.

Victor replied that the pampas was only one day from here.... I gulped, flushed and took a long pause to digest just what I thought I heard. What? I told him as clearly as I possibly could that I knew that. He had told us that yesterday.

It can't be. Surely, he didn't really say that. I was afraid of what that meant. I was struck dumb by the way he was pointing upstream as he said it. I didn't want to believe what I was thinking.

I quickly asked him how many days it would take to reach Puerto Maldonado. He looked puzzled, as if he wondered why I would ask a question like that.

It was time to cut the talk now and to get right to my worst fears. I pointed back at the river and asked if that was the Madre de Dios River. "Es que el Rio Madre de Dios?"

It wasn't. His eyes now opened wide, looking at me like I was some kid asking the teacher if I could skip class today. "No no, Señor, Rio Heath!"

I looked away to keep him from seeing how much I wanted to punch him in the snout. I turned to Bill, who had been fooling with some gear and not listening to this revelation.

"Guillermo, you will not believe this." I was trying to think how to tell him this. "You remember yesterday when we told the admiral here to turn around and head for Puerto Maldonado and even told him that we did not want to see the pampas?"

"Yeah, what?"

"You know how everything looked a little different today when we started back upstream?"

"No. He did not! You gottabeshittin me?? Are we heading for the pampas? Are we going up that other river? Damn." He was as awestruck as I.

"Yep, looks like it."

He gave me a half smile and jabbed, "So much for your Spanish, Señor Hammer.... Now what?"

Bill later fined me 100,000 Intis for being a "pisspoor" translator. I agreed to pay.

"Remember how wide the river was as we left? We were probably at the junction of the rivers where the Heath and Madre de Dios meet, and when he swung around to head upstream, he headed up the Rio Heath instead of the Madre de Dios, and we didn't know the difference. The map shows that the Rio Heath is the Peruvian-Bolivian border in some places and the pampas is way upriver on the Bolivian side. He still wants to show us the damn pampas. He had it in his mind that we were going there and he was the boss of this expedition. Or, maybe Tootsie told him that. I thought it was clear that we wanted to go back. I thought he agreed."

"Let's draw him a picture or something," Bill said. "Maybe I'll keep my hand on my knife while we talk to him. You sure he's not really related to Admiral Yamamoto, the guy that attacked Pearl Harbor?"

"Probably. He looks like him, especially with that hat we bought him."

"Maybe I'll turn his hat around backwards to remind him where we want to go."

"I don't know, Guillermo, but what if he gets embarrassed and thinks he has lost face, grabs your knife, and commits Harry Caray (Hara-kiri-ritual suicide) and we have to haul his dead ass back to Maldonado with just Peckahead Jose driving this boat?"

"Yep, that's out. Harry Caray—that's funny. "Holy Cow, hey, hey! and all that Chicago Cubs stuff. Wonder how Caray got to be a Cubs legend anyway."

I could see what happened. Having arranged this new jungle guiding enterprise with Fearis, she told him just what to do, where to take us, what to see, what to buy and I'm sure he wanted to do everything right. If she wrote to him as much as she did to us, all in Spanish, he would have been totally programmed by her. Our attempting to alter this plan confused him. He probably thought we didn't have a clue about what was going on, and of course our conversations are a bit strained anyway, so he stuck to his original plan from his "real boss," Tootsie.

There was no use flaring into some rage over that. The four of us had some serious traveling to do. It was easy to see why the admiral was insisting on following Fearis' instructions.

She was the one who arranged for the trip and the kind of trip he should take. It was no different with us. After all, she knew everything: what to take, what to see, what hazards and maladies we might experience, how we would get there and how knowledgeable the guides were. She was a woman, not a grizzled old swamp monster. How tough could it be? We had no real way of knowing our distance, degree of total isolation, and our risk exposure.

Victor and Jose, in our opinion, did not appear to have near enough provisions for a trip this long, and didn't really know exactly where they were going or how long it would take. These bozos might be good at a couple things, but we now knew not to trust them. As far as we were concerned, that made the continuation of this cruise even more dangerous.

One of the great ironies of exploration and settlement in the entire Amazon rainforest, the most bio-diverse area on earth, with the abundance of vegetation and animal species, has been the lack of any real life-sustaining foods. Many believe that this very difficult situation in acquiring the necessary foods has not allowed settling Indians or explorers the luxury of time to develop great civilizations, culture, arts, and sciences. There was no way to graze herds or cultivate crops, and not many of the thousands of plant species produce nutrition.

We now had to backtrack to reach the Madre de Dios River again and then pass by El Jefe's fully armed eagle's nest chugging upstream. What if, this time, he took some shots at us?

Bill would probably have fired me as translator if he could, but he couldn't. His Spanish was my only job security. This time I was going to have a real one-on-one with El Capitan, alone and with no smiles, jokes or misunderstandings. My mission was to get him to confirm back to me exactly what we were doing. He had to know that out here we were the jefes, the bosses—the paying customers—not Tootsie.

I pulled Victor aside, away from the campfire, for a separate conference. I sat on a pile of sticks, put on my sternest, but most friendly and understanding face, and we talked. He sat cross-legged on the ground. His head bobbed in agreement and understanding. He knew I was rejecting any and all of Tootsie's instructions and was ordering him to U-turn this boat and head for Puerto Maldonado early the next day and make minimum stops. He assured me he had plenty of fuel, but couldn't confirm that we even had enough provisions to extend this trip for more days.

I made sure to be as respectful, reasonable and understanding as possible. He knew I was deadly serious and paid close attention, repeated things to me, and we shook hands. We exchanged a couple of "muchisimas graciases" afterwards and I could see he felt the load of confusion lifted off his shoulders. Finally, we were amigos and had an understanding.

A quick thought shot through my mind. Tomorrow, if this little amigo captain happened to point to some place on the port side of this boat and said, "Mira, las pampas!" I would commit Harry Caray myself.

We crawled into our canvas two-man cocoon with the mosquito net windows, begged for some breeze, then thought about someday having an icy drink, a hot shower and a soft bed, all of which still seemed years away.

In our normal, bedtime pre-crashing conversation, Bill asked, "What did you mean the other day when you said we could die of appendicitis out here?"

I began seriously, "You could, you know. In fact, you could even be hacking some tree with that butcher knife of yours and a limb slaps you in the arm and that knife cuts an artery and those things spurt blood. I know very little about tourniquets and by the time we got you back to civilization you could croak from exsanguination."

"Ex —what?"

"Bleeding to death."

"Where did you get that word, Lipper?"

"Made it up. No, I just remembered it and wanted to use it someday. Never had a chance."

"What about appendicitis?"

"Guillermo, if you get appendicitis, and it bursts, you've got big trouble. Poisonous to the gut—fatal peritonitis. It has to be taken out and I would probably have to take your knife, sterilize it, cut you open. I do know about its location, halfway between the naval and hip. I would hope not to cut an artery. Then I feel around inside you 'til I find it, pull it out, tie a string around it and then cut it off, toss it and try to find a needle and thread..."

"That's enough, you hunyak. Got the picture. Let's get these midgets up early and get started back."

We sweated ourselves to sleep with the thought that Mañana, los dos gringo amigos with their Nipponese-Peruvian admiral and his crew, "Batman" Jose, are heading for the barn.

We hoped.

Chapter 15

Steaming Back

Very early the next day we made our u-turn and were headed downstream on the Rio Heath. The little pecke motor was at full throttle, faster than it ever ran before, and the boat wash was coming over the sides when we hit any small turbulence. We did not complain. It was a sign that this time, Victor got it.

It was late morning when we hit the wide Madre de Dios confluence and we swept far away from El Jefe's hill and remained mostly out of sight of his cabins. If he had anticipated our stopping on the way back from the pampas we were days ahead of anything he would have expected. No one saw us. Somewhere along the way we passed into Peru and began plowing upstream in the Madre de Dios, moving around the first island. This route also kept us far from El Jefe's view.

There was so much mud along this river that we had become more than a little tired of it. Lodo, lodo, lodo. It was silt or clay, very fine-grained and sticky. Step in it and the suction might keep your boot as you try to step out. Or you could slip and fall flat on your face. There were layers and layers of lodo in colors from red to blue, beige or gray and, of course, many shades of brown. We had no color preference for stepping in it from the boat, or walking on it or even washing dishes with it. Lodo was all the same.

Duck hunting in the Mississippi delta one time, I complained about the mud and a local good ol' boy told me, "This here Missipy mud is slicker 'n owl snot on a porcelain door knob." Yeah, probably, and it was the same here.

Growing up in the area near Cincinnati, I had walked around in some of the oldest clays and shales in geologic history. I knew that the red color meant oxidized iron content and that blue was unoxidized. We collected trilobite fossils from the Ordovician period. They were animals that lived hundreds of millions of years before dinosaurs. The only problem was that I never met many people who cared. Now was no exception. Even as interesting as the study of geology is, it can be a lonely lifetime hobby. As a cocktail party conversation killer, it ranks only one notch higher than gastroenterology.

The thick jungle vegetation and the tall trees all began to look the same to us every day, on both sides and around every turn of the river. The total lack of any trace of human intrusion, however, never stopped fascinating us. Not even radio waves or airplane contrails, and no possible way to know of news events in the world. We could actually be in World War III and we would have known nothing about it until we returned. In fact, it was at that very time in May 1990, while we were plying these waters, that Peru was undergoing a disastrous earthquake in the Alto Mayo region north of us. We had no idea. It killed sixty-five people, injured 607 and destroyed 3,000 houses, but we would never come to know a thing about it until weeks later when we were back in civilization. By then, it would be old news.

It was a kind of solitary confinement in wide-open spaces. We heard no familiar sounds, none we grew up with or currently lived with. We never heard the blare of a car's horn, the distinctive noise of an airplane, the mournful moan of a train whistle or any kind of music. Not even the whoosh of the wind. Bill and I remained on the lookout for big birds, monkeys and other animals. Most of them were inactive during the high-sun hours. When the birds were out, they did not show any fear of us since they had never been threatened by humans. Animals are very intelligent and alert to their threats. I recalled the ducks in Alaska, spooked at any human movement except for those fish-eating merganser ducks that might swim up to your boat. Since no one wanted to eat them, no one had ever shot at them, so they were not afraid.

Personally, and not secretly, I wanted revenge on that bold, nasty, unspeakable creature that took a dump less than two feet outside our tent that night, right next to our zippered exit. I swore never to put my bare hand on the ground again without looking. Now that I was armed with a serious bow and arrow, I had some sinister thoughts.

I told Bill and he laughed and said, "I can just picture you waking up, seeing the creature, unzipping the tent, going for the bow and arrows outside by the duffel, drawing it back, aiming and shooting. You would have to ask the damned thing if it would be willing to hold still for about fifteen minutes until you were done fumbling and ready to shoot."

On the next day, we loaded up early, snacked and moved out fast. At our first stop, we went through the forest for fruit and other edibles. The citrus and their so-called "limons," were available along with some other things. Victor picked something like big string beans. We knew we were to eat the pods, not the beans, but didn't.

It was a good moving day. Going upstream with the pecke-pecke motor wide open, we made a wake and some soaking splashes. It wasn't as tranquil as our coasting downstream had been. That little motor was screaming and running hot. We were plowing the water and leaving a wake.

Victor really showed off his river skills. He cut across bends, took interesting routes in calmer waters, dodged some V's in the stream that signaled troublesome rock obstacles, kept Jose busy in the bow and just generally hauled ass. It was impossible to tell how far we had come, but we were tired by dusk and camped closer to the river than usual, only slightly above the high-water marks on the trees.

A couple of those curiously disheveled jungle pheasants dropped in on us again. With wide-spread wings and tails fanned out, they dropped like small parachutists, crashing onto the limbs. Not at all like a smooth flying eagle, coasting in for a soft landing, with that light little lift to brake at the end.

Near where we were camped that evening, there appeared to be a giant bee or termite nest in the crotch of a tree about head high and thirty feet from where we were camped. It looked like a flour sack that someone had tossed in a tree. It was speckled and not as ball shaped as most of the termite nests. Right away Bill asked Jose if it was a killer bees' nest. Jose had no idea what he meant. I checked my dictionary and then chipped in with, "Abejas?"

"Si, abejas. Casa de abejas, si."

Well, he agreed. I added, "Killer bees? Killer abejas? Matador abejas?" I didn't know how to say killer bees in Spanish.

Jose got the idea. He said, "Si keeler bees, keeler bees, pero, nada mas." He said something like "Todos ellos se han ido."

He was gesturing that they had gone; it was an old abandoned nest. I just didn't want our Peckahead crewman to go up and beat on it and have either a surprise swarm of killer bees come out of hiding, or another squadron of bats.

Bill and I both said "OK, OK, that's good. No problema, no problema," and motioned for Jose to just sit quietly. A few minutes later, with a refreshing cup of Jose's finest tepid, riverwater cocktail in hand, I was curious, so I casually wandered over to the abandoned bees' nest to take a closer look. The speckled cover was a cover of live bees—very much alive—a swarm that covered the entire structure, just sitting there quietly humming, with only a little movement.

I told Bill so he wouldn't throw something at it.

Bill threw things a lot. Old pitchers do that. If I got hit by an old sock in the locker room, I knew who threw it. He threw a grape at me from another table during some big dinner once, caught me dead center in the head. Old catchers throw things back, so I found his grape and lofted it in return. No food fight or return volleys ensued, only the threat. Once upon a time, some of Bill's business associates arranged to have Bill throw out the first pitch at a Cubs game in Wrigley Field. He claims that he threw a strike. I have always been jealous.

We rose early the next day, ate little and started upstream as fast as possible, stopping only when necessary and for cooling the little engine. Bill hardly had time to whack many trees, and I didn't take many pictures.

All day we plowed upstream, around the long loops much slower than our trip downstream. Bill was better at spotting and counting those muddy caiman. I tried to take some bird photos. It was then that I really noticed the enormous variety of tree species that lived together in a rainforest. One usually expects to be in a pine forest or cypress swamp or to have some dominant species in the woods. Not here. There seemed to be dozens of different kinds of trees growing together, and vines that didn't care which one they would grow on.

On one of the outstretched arms of an enormous smooth-barked tree I noticed a thick vine that was growing around and over the limb that seemed to have a bark with a sort of pattern to it. It was brownish with lighter patterns that seemed to line up. I sort of followed it toward the trunk of the tree to see how big it was where it had climbed the tree. It suddenly came to a blunt end, one with a forked tongue shooting out from it, not far from some glassy, unblinking eyes. Oops, not a vine after all.

I snapped back six feet at supersonic speed. I couldn't identify it, but I didn't hang around for long trying to map its skin colors. I told Bill to go have a look at the strange vine I saw. He looked at me and somehow knew I was up to no good.

"No thanks, Hammer."

We steamed into the night, covering a lot of the river bends, and camped that night under a giant kapok tree, near its outstretched trunk. It seemed out of place, like a redwood in an orchard.

Talking to Victor, he thought that if we started temprano (early) y no problema we might be able to reach Puerto Maldonado by dark tomorrow. That would be a lot of miles. Early rising was definitely not a problem. Our tent was on a bump and a slant that night anyway. There could be chickens again at about 4:00 AM, so why not get moving. Getting back sounded good, even if it was to that varmint zoo they call a hotel. With the flashlight, I took my short look around at the pairs of red eyes for a caiman count. There were many, but I also looked at my skin for a quick moment and saw that I now had some red bumps, outlined in white, all over me. Now what?

Guillermo and I didn't talk much about how far and how many days it would still take to really reach home and safety. We were already a day late meeting our scheduled return and would have to catch another flight. We had lots of miles to even get to Maldonado. Thinking about it was not encouraging and wouldn't help a damned thing.

Bill said my red bumps didn't show much. They didn't itch. So what kind of bug bites you without being felt and then buzzes off without even leaving an itch?

I took a couple of antihistamine pills along with our regular malaria pills and went off to sleep as visions of sugared nuts danced through my head. Bill probably dreamed of the giant pintado he could have caught if he had brought heavier line.

Tomorrow was our final push. Beards were getting longer, we were less than clean and very hungry for something other than our depleting supplies. The next day I was going to take photos of things I may have missed and save only a few for Machu Picchu, in case we actually got there. I could have a good bug bite examination and scrub, even in that rusty, cold, dripping shower of the Hotel de Turistas.

A lot depended on this little fifteen horsepower two-cycle engine that was already working long hours, heating white hot and sipping a lot of fuel. The little paddles aboard would be good only for fighting our way through the flow of the river to get us to shore without capsizing.

We slid into our tent and bet each other on what time we would hear from some wildlife wake-up call.

Chapter 16

Dash for Home?

The alarm chickens were back at work at their usual 4:00 AM squawking, plus or minus a few minutes. They hardly waited for the sunrise. As usual, they crowed loud enough for us to believe they hated us, but they stayed out of sight, as well they should. We were hungry and would have loved nothing better than to turn these feathered alarm clocks into a chicken dinner.

Duffels were sloppily packed, tents torn down, Jose's settled boiled water skimmed for drinking and the motor warmed up, belching its usual oily smoke. Any paint or markings on the motor were burned off by now. It was a veteran pecke-pecke now. It had been "rode hard." Bill and I had our usual Pepto Bismol cocktail. Victor, as usual, took the tiller. Jose jumped into the bow and shoved off. Bill and I were on our plank, munching the last of the breakfast Brazil nuts.

Off the right side of the boat today would be parts of the jungle we had seen the least. The slope from the Andes fell toward the river on the left. Heavy forest trees lined both sides. We would not stop for termite nest inspections, ghost ship skeletons or jungle pillaging, only for necessary pit stops. With an all-out push, we might just reach that confluence with the Tombopata and that slippery mud bank at the foot of the hill, next to the thatched hut that was "the marina" at Puerto Maldonado.

We were disappointed in not seeing many of the interesting animals known to be native to the Amazon like the capybara, the largest rodent in the world, known to be three feet long and weigh over a hundred pounds. We did not see a sloth or step on an anaconda in the swamp, (which was really OK). Luckily, we missed seeing those little orange and black poison dart frogs. They say that the natives just touch their arrows to them and they become deadly weapons. We also missed seeing the harpy eagle. Maybe with luck we will be able to see the Peruvian national bird that lives in the Andes. It's named the cock-of-the-rock bird, big bird with an orange head and shoulders and a black body. We had also hoped to see some more of those strange South American monkeys too. Well, at least we saw thousands of parrots and a lifetime supply of their muddy "gators," the caimans.

The little motor that had served us so well so far was working hard upstream for a couple of hours. Then suddenly, it choked, farted loudly twice, then went silent.

Holy Hell! We had lost all power and steering. The river was boss now.

That immediately caused a major problem, as the current started to twist us sideways and would push us hopelessly downstream until we hit something or capsized. Jose kept busy with his pole, trying to keep us from turning sideways to the current while Victor panicked, busily yanking on the starter rope, red faced and sweating. Bill and I sat there staring at each other with the same thought—our worst nightmare was exploding into reality. There was no walking home from here.

How did we ever put ourselves in this vulnerable position? Yes, of course, we'd had second thoughts about this whole trip, but they were of no use right now.

We volunteered to help either of our crew with anything we could. Bill and I being side by side at midships, we couldn't lean over the side or both go to one side without causing us to flip. We couldn't help. We sat there like cheerleaders for our two little captors.

The boat was dangerously close to being sideways to the flow, a situation that would mean sure capsizing and spreading everything in this boat all over the river and, eventually, all down the muddy sides of the Madre de Dios for miles.

Bill and I grabbed a paddle and tried to straighten the boat. Considering the heavy weight of this boat, our efforts were fruitless. Water had not yet come over the sides. I quickly put camera and loose items in the duffel and zipped it. At least, if we were dumped into the water, everything would be in one bag. Bill did the same. We were just flotsam in this massive chocolate-colored flow, looking for some bank or tree to snag us, flip us and complete the nightmare. Without the usual sound of the engine, it was silent as we moved ever faster with the current.

After what seemed an eternity, our sweaty, red-faced admiral got a pop or two from the pecke engine as his arm was about to go numb. Then a second one, then smoke, then a full-throated roar as it began to run again. Maybe we were back in business! But not completely out of trouble—still moving sideways with the river flow, we had to be turned and propelled upstream without making some quick move that could flip us. Victor wisely headed for the center of the river where there was lots of water. There he started a long gentle turn of the bow upstream while continuing to be swept downstream, carefully maneuvering not to be snagged on a shallow bar or log.

I will never know how long that little episode took on the clock but it seemed an eternity. The number of thoughts per second that one can generate in that kind of panic is infinite. The little motor gave us one more thrill as it cleared its throat again, just to keep us on edge.

El Capitan straightened us out and began to make up lost distance, motoring happily by the areas we had blurred past during our panic. That was just enough of a slap across the face to get our attention and remind us of the kind of cruise we had booked, and pay homage to our Milwaukee idols, Stephen Briggs and Harold Stratton, for making this nice little motor.

These two gringo explorers would never again be so cavalier about planning an expedition. There should have been backup for everything. We should have been able to depend on the clarity of a common language, leaders' credentials and a lot of important details. The overriding risk was that we had taken ourselves completely out of all communication with the world. It seemed almost inconceivable that one could do that in 1990. It is a risk that the ancient explorers had to take but is no longer necessary.

A few long hours later, in mid-afternoon, we noticed more bird activity than usual. Large white herons moved from tree to tree. There were more songs, chirps, squawks and a few screeches. Were they celebrating our final run? We decided that maybe we were just in a more active area. "Pass the Brazil nuts, Guillermo." I held the camera at ready position. The formerly irritating chatter of the pecke-pecke engine had now become a symphony we wanted to hear played all day long.

By passing the areas where we might have stopped on the way downstream, we made good time going home. I was still able to get some different photos and notice a few things we hadn't really paid attention to before. Bill saw more caiman in the mud, and we saw more birds by traveling later in the day.

It was about 3:00PM that day when Guillermo, current holder of the title of Bill "Double Eagle" Lutz, on the golf course, pulled off another of his miracle feats. He nudged me and said, "You know, Liplock, we haven't had one of those famous heavy downpours here except for that short one at the village. I thought this was the 'rainforest.'"

"Guillermo, this isn't the rainy season. Remember, that is why we booked this in May?"

"I know, but it must rain other times too," he insisted.

Without an iota of exaggeration, and mindful of my unwritten, non-fiction contract demanding strict adherence to the truth, it was no longer than fifteen minutes from Bill's declaration, than a globe-covering, opaque black cloud appeared on the horizon, moving at us from the left—the southwest—to cover the sky like someone pulling up the blankets over your head. I looked at Bill in true amazement. It was becoming nearly dark as this monster cloud covered us. With a loud crack of lightning, the rain could be heard crashing through the trees on the left shore and then roaring across the water in torrents. It sounded like a waterfall as the leading edge rolled over us on the river. We scrambled to put on our parkas and cover as many things as possible with some tent material. During our dead motor scare I had already hidden the camera and other things that might need protection from the water.

Bill discovered that his new "Nam" jungle combat boots with the porous tops and holes to let perspiration out, worked both ways. He was soaked. His boots filled when the water was only two inches deep in the boat.

This was not like any rain we had ever seen. It was more like we were going under a waterfall than a rain shower. The drops, grouped into solid water balls, fell so thick that vision was impaired. The parkas were jokes. The sound of millions of large drops hitting the water made an uninterrupted crashing sound. We could feel the weight of all that water falling on us.

Every attempt to keep anything dry was futile. Water puddled on any fold of material, and flowed into any small opening. Nothing was dry under the parkas. They don't really work when someone has a fire hose on you.

The boat was starting to flood; everything in the boat was getting soaked from the bottom up. Victor passed us pots or cups to start baling before we sank. Bill and I, in the center of the boat, were at the lowest part, where all the water flowed. We worked hard and were throwing out water in a fury. We must have looked like a New York City fireboat on the 4th of July.

Keeping dry was no longer the objective. Keeping afloat was. After a while, I took a break from baling and caught enough rain to have a drink of it, no doubt the cleanest water we'd had in many days. It was delicious.

Victor kept on course somehow, even though vision was difficult. We gave him high marks for that.

After about thirty minutes, the rain stopped as the black cloud moved on. We were still fighting upstream. Finally, we were coming around the last big island of the river before the wide confluence with the Tombopata River. Bill and I looked at each other—soaked, bearded, wrinkled and exhausted. We had to laugh. At last, we broke into the mile-wide, buff-colored junction of the rivers. The sun was shining but preparing to sink behind the mountains far to the west. Heavy, wet tree limbs seemed to droop after their heavy down-beating. Daylight would last almost a half hour after the sun disappeared. Time enough to unload this watery canoe for the final time.

We turned left and soon found ourselves pulling up to our destination at the rain-soaked mudslide that was the Puerto Maldonado "marina" at the foot of the hill. We made it! Saturated, pooped, hungry, thirsty, spotted and dirty—but we're here. We just sat there for a while, smiling, exhausted. We gathered ourselves for the long haul up the hill.

Laboriously, we unloaded items from the boat. Small things first, trying to put them on boards or logs to avoid the mud. The duffels seemed to be twice their original weight, dripping water when raised. Our shoes squished as we stepped. I hoped the soaking hadn't ruined my film or the camera.

Where were all those eager villagers that were so happy to drag our stuff downhill on that sunny morning? Heavy, uphill and muddy proved to be a little different. After we had struggled up the slippery hill, a few of the little native kids helped us up the road, about the distance of one football field, to the hotel. That was worth a few well-soaked Intis tip, a fortune for them but well worth it. I wondered what they would do with the money. I found it ironic to be looking at this fleabag hotel as a treasured destination.

We were welcomed with a lift of one eyelid by the same droopy desk clerk we had left a couple of long weeks ago. He exhibited the same bristling excitement to see us this time as he did before. This "Host with the Most" yawned and tossed the two old keys at us for the same rooms, without saying a word.

It seemed that the rain had enhanced the familiar mildew odor and added a stale, smoky ingredient. Victor and Jose were also happy to have arrived and to go home. They promised to be back with a pickup truck in the morning to take us to the airport. But that would be the last we would ever see or hear of Admiral-boat-owner-guide Yarikawa.

We had missed our original flights so we would have to change our tickets and be on our way to Cuzco on the return leg of the same numbered flight that brought us. It was actually the only flight coming in and out of Puerto Maldonado from the civilized world, so we didn't have to worry ourselves about booking alternate plans. In spite of my new skin dots and hunger, it was a relief to make it back this far.

Bill and I were busy wringing out and hanging up as many of our things as we could. We grabbed all the hangers we could find (five) and hung up things on everything in our rooms that would hold something.

Just then, our old friend Mr. Anywho stuck his head in the room to welcome us back. It was great to see him. He looked at us and laughed. "Have a good trip?" He smiled at this pair of beaten, wet morons and we had to smile back.

"Yeah, great. You find El Dorado while we were gone?" I asked.

"Tell you about it later. Git dry and meet me up front."

Things hadn't gone that well at his gold mines. He had expected to leave days before this. With a big smile, he claimed to have made a big meatloaf and invited us to dinner during the generator hour. I couldn't remember anything that ever sounded better, unless it was on Christmas morning when I was five and Dad said, "Boys, let's go down and see if Santa came last night."

The rusty, dripping shower head, as bad as it was, seemed to sound better than standing barefoot in the muddy river throwing cold water over my head, but it wasn't. I was already soaked by the rain so a dry towel wipe down would have to do. I looked carefully at the red dots all over me, still with no idea what they were. I took another antihistamine, looked in the tiny mirror on the shelf and, shocked to see myself for the first time in many days, thought Body by Brazil Nuts. What an ad that would make. Probably kill the market for Brazil nuts.

We threw on some less damp clothes and joined our friendly international loner in the eating area. He wanted to know a lot about our trip before telling us what was going wrong with his gold mining partners.

It was past generator hour so we feasted on his meatloaf by candlelight as he related, as casually as he could, the personnel problems at his mines. People quit, some get into trouble, steal, loaf on the job, become ill or just wander away. He maintained that there should always be a question in the minds of workers just who in their midst is the company insider in the crew.

Supervision is everything, especially when the product is pure gold dust.

It was impossible for us to get any feel for how much money he made from these operations. We guessed that it was not a fortune. He was going out to one of the sites again tomorrow and maybe again the next day. We wished him the best and said that we expected to leave in the morning for Cuzco, a nice hotel, shower, wine, food and a clean soft bed.

His parting words were, "Well... anywho... gentlemen, nice meeting up with you and have a great trip back to the States. If you get to Australia, I gotta place near Newcastle in New South Wales. Look me up."

Back in my room #3, I had to smile at the laundry decorating every part of my room and how it was actually an improvement over the dark walls and open toilet/ shower corner of the room. It was too wet for the tap tap dripping of dew on the leaves outside that I remembered so well, but the rat-gnawing chorus was still working on something. By now they should have a giant pile of sawdust.

The bed was softer than the ground in the jungle and the room was better than the tent. After so long in the tent, I wasn't sure I could sleep without Bill's size-12s in my face, but I was going to try. What a great relief tomorrow would bring; a cool plane ride, Cuzco, a real hotel room, a hot shower, creature comforts.

Just thinking about it, we slept better than we had for as long as I could remember.

Chapter 17

The Nightingale Chickens of Morning

The alarm chickens started as usual at predawn but never sounded so beautiful. I jerked out of the sack with an extra shot of adrenalin—anticipating the trip to the airport, the ticket changes, escaping this hardscrabble jungle clearing and arriving in that beautiful Inca capital of Cuzco. Bill and I both started cramming our still damp things in the duffels. We dressed, then dragged things to the front, where Jose and his helper threw them into the bed of the same red dust-covered pickup truck we recognized, but the dust was now mud. We grabbed a granola bar from our nearly depleted stash, took care of the room bill, joking with the zombie clerk hopelessly trying to arouse a glimmer, a grin, something, gave up and climbed into the truck bed. In a cloud of lodo and a hearty "Hi-yo Silver" we were off to the airport, trying to ready our tickets and paperwork.

The usual dust wake was actually a spray of mud since the heavy rain of the day before. We bounced and splashed our way through the puddles in the road, looking back on this failed little settlement now as an experience that we were glad to have had, rather than the depressing line of shacks that we saw on the way in. We were leaving. We took in the sights of the drive to the airport with experienced truck-riding skills wrapped in excitement about the trip to Cuzco.

The truck pulled up in front of a nearly vacant little airport building. Not much went on there as we unloaded the truck. Jose went into the building, came out and started throwing bags back into the truck, muttering "cancelado, cancelado." A small handwritten sign on the side of the building read, "Vuelo 432 cancelado." We weren't going anywhere. No reason given for the cancellation. If there were any other hopeful passengers, they had already gone by now. There was no airplane on the ground and none expected.

Bill and I stared at each other for at least a minute, considering our new misfortune, our dashed plans and what to do about our dilemma. The only possible option was perfectly clear to Jose as he had nearly finished throwing all the bags back into the pickup. He waited until we climbed aboard and we were off again, back to the not so beautiful Hotel de Turistas, that 0.3-star resort down the Avenue de Lodo. The very thing we never wanted to see again except in my photos. The never-surprised clerk checked us in again, tossing us the same keys to the same rooms, as Jose waited to see what we might plan to do for the rest of the day.

Mr. Anywho had already left for the mines. We were stuck here for another night.

Jose let the local transport pickup truck go. He remained with his little motor scooter in front of the hotel. We finally decided that we should probably decorate our rooms again with all our damp clothes. The various autumn shades of mold were not "in" this season. This day and all night might actually finish the drying, or close enough. We let Jose go home, with the promise that he would return tomorrow for another try. We sat, read and took a short walk around the outside of the hotel.

We noticed a small palm tree had been planted near the weathered wooden stairs in front of the porch exactly where a gigantic anthill had stood before we left. A close look revealed that the ants were still there, furiously running around, highly pissed off, and not willing to relocate.

It is fascinating to watch ants work, scurrying around in lines, carrying things larger than they were. They were not willing to accept this tree without reorganizing and rebuilding. They were not leaving their ground.

On the side of the hotel, in tall weeds, we spied a large hole lined with concrete and partially filled with a pile of leaves in various stages of decay. It was an obvious attempt to build a small swimming pool. It was bowl shaped, about twenty feet in diameter. We wondered when it had come to the attention of their marketing geniuses that with only muddy river water, no electrical pump and few if any guests, a pool was not really going to be a main attraction for new tourist business. We had a good laugh. There wasn't a diving board, anyway.

Having both had our starts in the business world in marketing, Bill and I agreed that, for starters, the hotel owners should first give serious consideration to installing a flush toilet. But then, what the hell do we know about the hotel business?

We decided to see the town, as long as we were stuck here— maybe buy some post cards or something. When we asked how far it was to the main street, we found that we were on it. The rest of the town was up the dirt road. Bill, intent on taking a shower or bath somewhere, grabbed his little athletic bag of undies and Dopp kit and off we walked.

There were no motored vehicles in town. There were old bicycles and some pull carts with bicycle type tires on them. There was an open-air market with piles of bananas, squash and corn. All the people were from native tribes, short, wide-faced, dark complexioned, with black eyes and bushy black hair. Their clothes were colorless and looked old and wrinkled. Most looked worn and dirty as you might expect in a place without electricity for heat, pumps and all other appliances. Half the men were barefoot. The women all wore skirts or housedresses and flat shoes. No make-up or fancy hairdos of any kind. It is difficult to know from what tribes or settlements the town's inhabitants had come, or when. The official language in Peru is Spanish but I am sure that many in this town spoke Quechuan or something.

Somewhere along the road, a small, ugly, black pig looked us over and took a real liking to Bill. I never found out why. Was it his looks, dress, smell, or the way he walked? Maybe his nose? The pig was right at his heels the whole time. I was crumpled up laughing but Bill wasn't. Maybe he was used to having pigs follow him around. If we went into some building, the pig would wait for him to come out. If Bill crossed the road, the pig followed.

It didn't have any interest in me. My feelings weren't really hurt, really, just curious. Since I had the camera, maybe he thought I was just the papparazzo.

I laughed myself into a sweat and took snapshots for evidence.

That escapade joins the fishing story of his throwing the hook, leader and bait into the drink, as one more story I would not promise to keep secret. I knew he was going to tell about my hand in the midnight phantom's huge turd and my lousy command of Spanish or my poor archery.

Bill's piggy wasn't even cute. It had a long snout and a black messy coat of hair. The only good thing I could think to say about it was that it didn't fart or bite.

We couldn't find many little wooden stores open for business. There were open doors, no clerks and one store with a big sign over it reading, "COMMERCIAL FANNY." That gave us absolutely no clue to the nature of their business. A store that displayed postcards wanted a fortune for yellowing cards that were thirty years old and looked it. They could not have sold any since the day the store was built. The price was about Inti 1.50 each. That seemed outrageous so we gave them twenty-five cents and told them they were lucky to get that. Something passing for a post office occupied the corner of one store. They didn't have any business but displayed some official looking rubber stamps and a slot for letters. The clerk had no idea how many estampas to use. "Es posible, seis." Well, if they thought six would do it, eight would do it better. So, we went ahead and put on eight stamps, wrote our notes and mailed them to family back home, expecting to reach home before they did.

Dinners in the local restaurants cost less than these cards.

Out in this jungle the international exchange rates for currency did not enter into local commerce. Everyone dealt in Intis as a medium of exchange, and each "businessman" offered his own valuation. It mattered little whether inflation had made the Inti worth a fraction of a U.S. dollar in the international marketplace. A dozen eggs costs one Inti—yesterday, today and tomorrow. What do today's currency exchange rates matter if you're not exchanging currency? That, of course meant that the $150 worth of Intis I gave to our guides for provisions was a bonanza for them in buying power here in the jungle town and why he never asked for more—and why I never got any change. One look at these people told me that no one was going to fight for any small change back out of $150.

As we walked along, we encountered a fat, toothless woman sitting by the side of the road next to a small sign that said "zoo." I was amazed to catch sight of a young boy in the doorway of one of the shacks, holding a beautiful jaguar cub in his arms as if it was his little brother. The cub's clear amber eyes gazed out at any action from the safety of the boy's arms. Its white fur was covered with spots of black with yellow centers. This little

The native boy with his "pet" jaguar cub.

armful of jaguar had very large paws, a hint at the size he would attain someday.

Bill and I immediately guessed where he could possibly have found this cub and what happened to its mother. I wanted to pet it, but not if mama jaguar was anywhere on the loose. I would definitely be identified as a stranger to her. I couldn't see her. Then, while Bill stood there petting the cub, I happened to look down. Looking me in the eye from halfway under the shack was a full-sized jaguar, a beautiful animal of two hundred plus pounds of muscle, lightning speed and a famous bite. I smiled while I gently nudged Bill to the side, away from the boy and his cub, whispering to him not to make any quick moves. Bill understood. Mama stayed still, but continued to watch our every move.

Our toothless guide then beckoned, encouraging us to come between the shacks to see something else. We followed her and saw piles of small and large cages all crammed together. It appeared to be a major snake collection. Wide wire cages only six inches in height were stacked from the ground up to about eye level. Each contained a large snake—large tree boas, striped boas, vipers and a whip snake. Some of the other colorful striped snakes I couldn't identify. I did recognize, in one huge cage, an anaconda, the monster of South American snakes. He had a still, non-blinking stare and a forked tongue darting out. It was a scary feel.

The acrid stench of these serpents and their poop was so bad that it made our eyes water. It was the first time I ever felt sorry for a hissing, mean-looking snake. These cages were in the dark, smelly, allowing the animals to raise their heads only about four inches, with no opportunities for real moving or climbing. It was serious confinement. These were wild animals and this seemed cruel. A couple more cages housed what looked like large rodents. Maybe food for the snakes.

We made our way back to the boy with the jaguar, dropped an Inti in a box that obviously was built with a slot just big enough for an Inti bill, took a photo and left. The baby jaguar was an adorable pet, if it could only stay a cub and not grow up.

Jaguars are the third largest cats, behind lions and tigers. They look like leopards but live like tigers, including their shared ability to swim. Their bite is extremely powerful for a cat. They can crack open the armor of reptiles, even sea turtles, and usually kill their prey by crushing the skull. I got a headache just thinking about mama jaguar—and her powerful jaws—staring at us from under the shack. I took her picture, and one of the boy and his cub, then moved away.

When we returned to the hotel, Mr. Anywho was completely surprised to see us still in Puerto Maldonado. We met again for meatloaf, a partial glass of horrible red wine, rice and something else not worth remembering. He explained to us that flight cancelations here were not unusual. No surprise.

He reminded us, "It costs that little Aero-Peru airline a lot of time, fuel and manhours to fly into this little place. In fact, Aero-Peru is probably one of those nationalistic ventures losing money. It seems every country has to have its own airline and its own steel mill to keep up their show of sovereignty and self-reliance (and because their neighbors have them). Carrying three or four passengers, they lose a lot of money and just won't do it. Hell, they know you'll be here.... Gents...you are captive. You might have the same thing tomorrow, 'cause they don't care a damn bit about you. And, there ain't no other way outta here anyway... well, anywho... there's tomorrow."

An uncomfortable silence followed. We knew he was right. He added, "I'll wait and see if you make it tomorrow. If not, maybe you would like to go out to the mine with me. Anywho, we'll see tomorrow."

That wasn't good news. What if Aero-Peru decided to cancel service here again and again or forever? We knew of no other way out of here. There was a rumor of an old trail cut through from the mountains that would someday provide overland access, but even then it would take days, requiring fuel, food, tents, weapons, brush cutting equipment and who knows what else. Turns out it was only a mule trail, never really used. It was not really an option of any kind.

Our usual annoying chorus of dogs, chickens, and rat chewing, punctuated by the usual loud squawk, serenaded us to sleep again. Rather than becoming more accustomed to this music, we found it even more chafing. Besides, I was beginning to feel feverish, achy symptoms like oncoming flu. The mirror showed a few more of those mysterious red dots with white halos breaking out on my skin. I had heard of dermatitis from soap. What about dermatitis from lack of soap? I took some more antihistamine but also thought it was worthwhile to start that generic antibiotic, Keflex, that I had always carried with me overseas.

If tomorrow didn't bring us an airplane, we would really have to do some serious planning.

Chapter 18

Second Try

The first sound I heard in the morning, after the screaming alarm chickens, was Bill, three rooms away, growling as he jammed things in his duffel. I got busy. We dragged our tired luggage down the hall to the front, where Jose and his helper were waiting to load the pickup—again. We checked out—again—jumped in the truck bed—again—and bounced and swayed our way to the airport— again—only to be confronted by that same sign on the outside of that wretched airport shack that said "CANCELADO." Again.

We could find no one in the building to question about anything. We stood in a puddle of total frustration, just sort of gazing around. We had no thoughts, no options, not even someone with whom to commiserate. Bill and I looked at each other, said nothing and climbed back into the pickup.

Bill said, "Think about it. This could happen every day, forever—and there is no one here to tell us anything, and no one else in this town to tell us anything."

Back at the hotel, we signed in again and were greeted by our smiling Mr. Anywho, not surprised to see us. He offered to fill our extra day of captivity with a ride to his gold mine near the town of Labertino, a small settlement not that far from here, or so he said. We unpacked and hung up anything still damp,

But before we left, I said that I wanted to try the telephone at the desk to see if we could get a line out. Sleeping Beauty, our zombie at the desk, told me that a call was only possible during generator time and we could come back later. I had the international numbers for the U.S. and for Gibbs, the agent in Chicago who had made our reservations. If Gibbs couldn't do something, at least someone back there would be aware of our plight and maybe could get us out.

We decided to go with Mr. Anywho this afternoon and maybe try the phone later. Anywho, not full of good news, casually advised us that he had never gotten a line out when he was here. Somehow, Mr. Anywho had commandeered the town pickup truck and we piled in. As he climbed into the passenger side, he said we could get a bite to eat when we got there. We jumped into the truck bed, grabbed our favorite overhead pipe rack and were off to the mine, still thinking of the time when we would leave this whole rainforest behind us. For the entire time we rode in pickup trucks, we rode only standing up and shifting around as we bounced and swayed. It was never relaxing in any way. This town of Labertino was supposedly 34 miles away. It would be the longest 34 miles either of us had ever traveled, not to mention that there was a boat trip to take after we got there.

– The Gold Mine Gauntlet –

Our truck bed-riding skills and callouses, so well developed by now, were going to be fully tested today. This ride was long and getting longer. We were hours into this trip with no idea when we might ever arrive. Mr. Anywho, knowing what a rough ride this was, had stopped twice to give us a break from the gripping, dipping and bouncing so we could rest, maybe water a bush, have a drink of water and climb aboard for more. It ceased to be fun or interesting, became uncomfortable and was heading, fully, toward seriously painful. For hours we lurched and bounced on this road consisting of two tire tracks in a shrinking tunnel of vegetation that seemed to be closing in on us by the mile. Much too late, we discovered this trip was going to take three and a half hours one way in the pickup truck. We lurched and bounced along while getting smacked with overhanging limbs and vines for the entire ride.

We finally stopped at a row of shacks on a river's edge while Anywho got out, with wallet, and visited one of the shacks, returning in a couple of minutes. As in Bolivia, it was an unofficial toll but, like something in medieval Europe, it helped with local native relations, which was critical.

With cramped hands and arm muscles from hanging on, we climbed out of that truck and were pushed toward a boat for the next leg of the trip—upriver, through nothing but jungle, for nearly an hour to a shallow part of the river where a series of pipes, pumps and waterflow created the placer mine. Sweaty, dark-skinned native men shoveled rocks, gravel and mud. After a washing system that seemed complicated, two men carefully watched for gold as the sediment crossed a black velvet-looking area on a conveyor belt, into a catch basin and from there back into the river. The catch basin seemed to act as a second chance if something slipped past the last examination—like an, "oops-have-another-look" basin.

An open-sided shelter covered by a thatched roof served as headquarters, a lunch hall and baño for the workers with a few tables and chairs and a fire pit just outside. It was close to the river so it was built on stilts. The unique and remarkable feature of this building, that Bill and I will never forget as long as we live, was the existence of an open-air porcelain toilet mounted on a plank of the floor. It was extended and cantilevered beyond the floor, outside the shelter. It looked like a toilet on the end of a diving board, without the water tank. The latrine pit was below.

Anyone using this spectacular and unique diving board throne would have no privacy. He would not only be fully visible sitting there beyond the thatched roof overhang but his bombardment could be duly noted by anyone who wished to watch such a production. This added a new wrinkle to plumbing history and to the old expression, "walking the plank."

I am sure the workers must have lived in deadly fear of accidentally seeing it in use. Even worse might be to have the plank break off while using it. Bill and I were willing to endure excruciating pain to avoid using it that day.

Oh, it should be noted that no women worked at this site.

A late lunch was finally served in this open-air structure— rice and bananas, for a change! —complete with an invasion of a squadron of wasps, bees, and swarming flies. Bill wore a yellow shirt, which was exactly the wrong thing to wear when bees are around. They loved him. He didn't know whether to swing his arms at them and have them sting him or leave them alone and risk having them land on him, crawl around and maybe sting him anyway.

He did a little of each and got by with only one sting. He was more than a little annoyed and let us know it with some choice verbiage. He even reused a couple of those strong expletives we had previously reserved for Jose and Victor.

Must have worked. Only one sting, and he didn't cry.

Without knowing, someone might think that watching a placer gold mining operation in a river would be somewhat exciting. Sorry, but it is a monotonous, mind-numbing exercise. We watched the placer mine operation for a while, then piled back into the boat and headed downstream toward the truck.

During this return boat ride, we were deluged by another surprise cloudburst that soaked our only remaining dry clothes.

They almost dried again, however, during the final couple of hours of the excruciating truck ride to Puerto Maldonado. Bill, being taller than I, took a much harder beating from overhanging limbs and leaves. The truck cab bends them back and they whip forward and down, slapping you if you are too high. I couldn't help wondering how the shocks and springs in that truck could have taken that pounding.

Rather than offering us a pleasant day of relaxation, this had been an endurance test. We were more than worn out. It was difficult to imagine how Mr. Anywho would consider this something fun for us to do since we were stuck in town. After some late, cold chow by candlelight, we fell comatose under our musty covers until the ear-splitting chicken alarms cut loose at sunup.

Chapter 19

A Grand Evening

We had decided to go earlier to the airport the following day so that if the flight was canceled again, we might at least be able to learn something more about this deteriorating and seemingly hopeless mess at the airport and our prospects of not spending eternity in this little town of Puerto Maldonado. We would be able to grab the airline people—or someone—and find out something. I had some Spanish sentences ready.

A tightening sense of entrapment that I had never felt seemed to squeeze my chest in a vice grip. We were stuck in the wrong place. Puerto Maldonado seemed to be a name that might literally be translated as "Cursed Port." Mal donado means "bad gift." Maldonado may have been a man's name, but in Spanish it often means "bad guy." Take your pick. I wondered if we should have done our homework on omens.

We were also sick of Hotel de Turistas and all its 0.3-star rating, which we now considered a little generous.

Throwing our stuff in the pickup truck again was a sore muscle chore. This was the third time to the airport and, we were confident, would be the charm. Our last goodbye to Mr. Anywho had been for real. We had seen our last placer mine. We were even nice to the lethargic sleepwalker at the desk, whom we never expected to see again.

This ride to the airport was like the first day, bristling with the thought of taking off for Cuzco in a dry, cool airplane. The bouncy pickup truck couldn't repress the anticipation of the high, dry and cool capital of the ancient Incas, a real hotel, maybe even hot water for the first time in what seemed like years. Even a third-rate hotel would be a gangbuster, dynamite, first-class upgrade. There seemed to be no way we could be marooned here longer. We were going to go!

At the airport there was no plane on the ground except for those dilapidated, old red biplanes over by the trees, probably bought as crop dusters or something. We were early. The incoming flight from Cuzco apparently had not arrived yet. Many more people milled around this time, all restless natives. After at least three days of cancellations, the passengers were increasing in number every day. There was only one way to leave this hole in the trees, and that was this single flight to Cuzco.

This small crowd of native bindle stiffs was not a happy lot. Voices were peaking. One man pounded angrily on the closed door of the building as if it would suddenly open and solve his problems.

The door did open, but not to let people in. Two small, sloppily uniformed guards held the door as a man in his street clothes put out that hated sign. CANCELADO.

The noise got louder. Bill and I felt totally helpless. We couldn't find anyone to talk to. No one would open the airport shack's door for anyone. We could not even think about where to go. We were in the same fix as yesterday. Jose just looked at us. Two big foreigners in wrinkled clothes, standing there in the red dirt, next to the dust-and-mud-covered pickup, in our imprisonment, without communication, electric power, translators or anyone who could assist us.

Rather than a disappointed look, Jose wore the face of a man watching his puppy just lying there mortally wounded. He glanced at the sky, then back at us, shrugged his shoulders, and calmly waited for us to give him the sign to sling our bags back into the truck.

Beyond anger now, Bill and I stared at each other, our brains grinding out only sawdust, not even a helpful curse word. A dark thought bounced around in both our minds—that we might be in deeper trouble than we thought. During my years of traveling, I had missed planes, lost a passport, had a wallet full of everything stolen. I had survived being broken down in cars, delayed or cancelled by planes and lost in cities, but never had I experienced such a total brain vacuum. It was a solid blank wall. The only option we had was to go back to the same hotel, try to use its phone during generator hours to call someone, somewhere, for something. We were back in the truck, back to the flea-bag hotel. The one to which we had so joyously bid good riddance—three times already.

Once again, I made enough noise to summon the desk slob and begged him to get an outside telephone line. The phone was dead. No explanations were offered; no alternatives were suggested.

Mr. Anywho was gone. Where did he go? How? There were no planes, boats or other means of escape that we knew of. He may have known someone nearby and was holed up there. Maybe he was dead and buried. Wherever he was we were never to see or hear from him again. Mr. Anywho was missed. He was our only experienced, visitor here, our only English-speaking consolation. We hadn't really tapped all his ideas for escape, and now he was gone.

I guessed that Brazil nuts were not brain food. Who's to say this can't continue happening every day? Even if a plane comes in, what are the chances we can get on it? There was now a backlog of angry natives—Spanish-speaking people waiting now in numbers that will more than fill the seats of any plane that comes to this hole-in-the-jungle. In this situation, how good are the chances of a couple of gringos working this out and getting on a plane ahead of a mob of angry natives that grows in number every passing day? The occupants of this little airline office merely hung up a sign announcing a cancellation and disappeared from the face of the earth. I had no idea how to make our case to the airline people, if we were even able to see them. Probably the same chance Guillermo had of landing that angry 200-pound pintado on his little collapsible bluegill rig.

Every day we had gone through the same routine of going to the airport. It hadn't worked out. We were reliving the same day, every day, with the same failure. It would be three years later that someone would make a movie called "Groundhog Day" that would remind us—painfully—of this frustration.

We were back in this hotel with every one of its discomforts that we had been so happy to leave an hour before. We knew that Jose was sorry we had not left, but another side of Jose was showing now. He could read the anguish and frustration on our solemn faces as we bounced around in the pickup. He was actually helping us to be more comfortable, as he looked after our bags and especially our local transportation. We hadn't looked at him as much more than a safety hazard for most of the trip. But now, we realized his worried facial expressions were sincere. He stayed with us a little longer than usual and offered to show us a place for lunch.

With no better idea, we went with him in his kind of rickshaw-wheelbarrow combination he pulled with his scooter. Bill and I had to laugh, imagining the sight of these two big gringos in the back of a homemade crate being pulled down a dirt road by a small man on a tiny Honda scooter.

Many of the little things he did were far beyond any duties or obligations he might have had as a guide. He was our friend now.

The restaurant sported a homemade sign that said Danubio Azul. I recognized it as one that Tootsie had included in her vast ramblings. It was painful to even think of an eatery in this sweltering jungle that would have the temerity to call itself "Blue Danube." This had to be worth a few smiles.

The screened porch dining area had table coverings of old oilcloth. Their china was actually a mixture of plastic with some paper items. Their crystal pieces were high mileage, well-etched plastic, and the silverware was picnic quality soft stainless—one fork, one knife. Unfortunately, without electricity, there was not even a fan. We just sat, sweated, chewed and sipped warm, fizzy bottled water as we were entertained by the ubiquitous canine and poultry concert. As I sat there perspiring, staring out in space, above that scene, above the cordillera horizon, I kept thinking about how few people in this world would ever suspect that a commercial airline destination existed on this earth that could not be reached by any other means of transportation— no roads, rail or boat service—and had no electrical power and only a rumor of limited telephone service. I wondered if there were any other towns like this anywhere in the world.

The fish actually tasted good, a dorado—a real improvement from piranha. Even the rice was good. We thanked Jose when he hauled us back to the hotel. As he left he said something about returning for tonight for some "Lugar especial para noche" or something. Lugar especial? A special place for night?

Bill and I had a serious discussion about our alternatives and what we might try for getting out of here. It was like sitting down to a table with a pencil, paper and a coffee to list our alternatives—and drawing a compete blank. There were just no people speaking English, and we could hardly get to anyone at the airport. The passengers we saw nearly rioted at the sight of anyone who might get them a seat if a plane did come.

We settled on trying again tomorrow. Failing to get a plane, we would try to tackle some airline person. Failing that— and we fully expected to fail—we'd return to the hotel and sit by the phone until we could get a line out. With the help of "Whiz-bang" the half-asleep desk zombie, maybe we could contact the U.S.A. in some way and then maybe get the travel agent, Gibbs, in Deerfield, Illinois. She was a friend and an experienced travel agent. She may be able to carry our story through airlines, consulates or whatever. We even toyed with the thought of going door to door in Puerto Maldonado to try to find an English-speaking person that might at least point us in the right direction to find a phone or talk to an airline person. Door to door in this seemingly impoverished place might lead to some violent encounter or something else disagreeable if not downright lethal. And why would someone who speaks English live here? We would at least need Jose to assist us in something like that.

Our dilemma here was beginning to look like a treadmill to nowhere. Being totally out of touch in every way, we might be in the midst of some world event and not know it. In this town, we could locate no government facilities—no help that we could find.

I sat and worked on some Spanish sentences and questions I would use, if possible.

Bill and I weren't sure how much weight we had lost on this trip, but it was not as much as it might have been if it weren't for those bags of Brazil nuts. Our peanut butter and granola bar supply was long gone. Mr. Anywho did not return that evening, so Bill and I went to the eating nook in the hotel to see what we could order. There was Jose, smiling and urging us to grab a couple pieces of bread and come ride with him in his rickshaw. We did.

After sundown, the only light in this town came from the moon or some shack with either an oil lamp or candle. That night there was no moonlight. It was starless, a ride out into the pitch-black. The two of us sitting jammed in a small wheelbarrow type of rickshaw was at least a different kind of uncomfortable from a pickup truck bed. We gradually learned new shock-absorbing skills.

The ride was long. We were far out of town riding behind a tiny scooter with a very dim headlight. No landmarks, buildings or other manmade objects. We were on a completely dark, uninhabited stretch in a half swampy, half jungle no-man's land. This was dangerous, but neither of us mentioned it.

I couldn't help thinking how completely vulnerable we were to disappearing without a trace. What did we really know about Jose other than he tried to kill us with river water and rabid bats? Would he dump us into a swamp for our unsigned travel checks and a couple Intis? Couldn't be worth it...could it?

We finally pulled up to a cleared area where, in front of us, stood a metal barn—the first structure of its kind we had seen. We went inside the small door. The barn boasted a bare concrete floor and echoed like an empty warehouse. How did this get here? The owner came up to greet us and ushered us to a classic wooden A-frame picnic table. We sat down.

"Cerveza mis amigos?"

"Si, dos. Bill, we're having a couple beers."

Valasquez was the owner and very proud of this building. He plopped down two large photo albums showing the complete step-by-step construction of this barn, from beginning to end. Valasquez leafed through the photo album as if he was a steel building salesman showing us every panel and bolt. It had to have been shipped in by boat, but from where? How?

Down the length of this barn were rooms on both sides where normally you would expect horse stalls. Instead of a hay mow above them, an open space. Each room had its door ajar, with a little light coming from it. There were about a dozen rooms altogether.

Jose took no time in pointing out that there were Señoritas in each room. "Chicas, mujeres. Echar un vistrazo? Le gusta?" (You like it?)

He seemed in a hurry to have us approve of this jungle bordello. It must have been his favorite, and we were his enablers. I tried to assure him that we would take a look but he should go ahead with his visit to where he was heading. He must have felt comfortable leaving us with our picture album and our beer as he strode off to one of the stable doors that he seemed to know quite well.

It was all that Bill and I could do to keep from choking, just trying to hold back a huge belly-laugh at this whole thing. You couldn't make this up. We decided to bet on how long it would take Jose to finish his frolic with his favorite. We bet 1,000 Intis, over or under twelve minutes. I took "over" and Bill took "under." At precisely eleven minutes and ten seconds on my watch, Jose reappeared at our picnic table, a contented chessy-cat grin on his face.

I lost.

Jose began pulling us to at least have a look. There were "muchas damas, muchas buen sexos. No problemas. Una mirada. OK?"

By now, Bill and I were dying to look inside these little doors at the merchandise. In each there was a stocky native girl, well, woman, heavily made up, sitting in a chair beside a bed in front of a dresser that had lots of bottles of make-up, nail polish, perfume, and who knows what. Dozens of things cluttered the room. All of the women were short, stubby, wide-faced and never once looked at us. They obviously had no marketing and sales promotional skills whatsoever. They were always busy doing something, as if we didn't exist. Was that some kind of sexy in their minds?

"Hey, Bill, they act like they don't want anything to do with us. Think that the style here is for hookers to play it hard-to-get?"

We crumpled up laughing. A nearly vacant jungle brothel with indifferent hookers? Wish I had my camera.

It was far from a beauty contest—maybe more like a 4-H show minus the feeding troughs and curry combs. Surprisingly, we saw no body parts hanging out, no nudity of any kind. Made one think that none of them had anything they were proud of, which was quite possible.

The funky, floral perfume smell from each room was overwhelming, nose biting. The wardrobes presented the most unbelievable element. One woman must have thought it was sexy to have stockings rolled down to just below the knee. Another had a slit skirt with garter belt showing. A slit skirt on a short-legged native is a miniskirt and actually measures only inches long. Inch-long eyelashes on small, fat faces just "don't git it" either. Porky's wife, Petunia? This was like being backstage at Ringling Bros., sans the red noses.

Bill posed the question, choking back a laughing outburst, "Do you think they all have day jobs, and this is just an odd job for some extra spending money? Like maybe brain surgeons or stock brokers?"

Bill and I must have permanently bruised ourselves elbowing each other to look at this one or that one, and not laughing.

A couple of bouffant hairdos looked like black space helmets. We couldn't imagine how this many women could come here each night, sit here with virtually no traffic, and make any kind of a living. If only we had been able to take pictures of each one. What a great catalog it would make. Their feigned indifference to potential customers was a perfect comedic touch.

It was tough to keep a straight face and pretend that we were really shopping. If I heard Bill snicker, I would have to hide my face to suppress a convulsive laughter breakout. I still smile just thinking about it.

It was difficult, socially speaking, to shake our head no at each doorway as if we were impressed but just not totally sold, but we managed to make it through. I decided how to let Valesquez know we just couldn't indulge. I figured how to say "No thanks, but we are married," in Spanish, so I put on my most pained, regretful face and said, "Los sientos, estamos casados."

To which he quickly replied, "No problema, nosotros tambien." They were married too. So what?

I gave Velasquez some Intis (they are virtually worthless) for which he thanked us. We grabbed some snacks and laughed our way home in the rickshaw, bruising our butts and talking about the unique display of feminine pulchritude we had been afforded this evening. We don't know what our satisfied Jose thought of us, because we were too busy laughing to care. A bordello in a homemade barn with the lounge on a concrete floor and furnished with a semi-comfortable wooden, A-frame picnic table? Who'll believe us?

I reminded Bill that from now on, when we come to a picnic location at some park and spot an A-frame picnic table, we can honestly say, "Well, they have decorated this park like a whore house."

Right now, nothing really mattered except getting out of this jungle prison.

We felt a little sad for Jose. He was trying his best to make our delay less painful. We thanked him sincerely, including pats on the back, handshakes and all the graciases we could muster. He was really trying to help.

It was another dank, smelly night in Hotel de Turistas with its usual dark noises. One might think we were used to it by now. Not so. We were sick of it but couldn't help laughing.

Maybe tomorrow? And our after-failure plan.

Chapter 20

Slammed

A t first rooster call, Bill moaned and exclaimed, "Hey, my stuff finally dried, almost. What about yours?" Our rooms closer together now, and with no other visible occupants around, we could yell at each other while we crammed the same clothes back into the same tired luggage.

I checked for more red spots. No new ones and the old ones were fading. Check-out was now totally routine. Sleeping Beauty at the desk decided to be humorous today, slurring a lazy, "Hasta luega." Like we were coming back later.

"We hope not, Sleepy. This time we're outta here."

We threw our stuff back in that familiar muddy truck bed, climbed in and bounced our way back to the so-called airport. The ride was getting longer and more worrisome. Swapping our tickets for new ones, getting continuing seats to Lima in a day or two, luggage transfer and who knows what other delays were tasks that we had no idea how to accomplish.

It didn't take long to raise our curiosity as we neared the airport. No airplane again. Well, maybe it hadn't arrived yet.

Maybe just delayed. We weren't leaving until we could talk to someone at the airport, if we had to physically pin them on the ground.

That thought quickly vanished too when we saw the familiar "Cancelado" sign. This time it said, "no vuelos" and the airport was abandoned, office and all.

That prompted our chorus of "Aw shit!" This was our most ominous rejection so far. Not even anyone to question–about anything–in any language. I think we stood there looking at each other for what seemed like an hour. Probably only ten seconds, but with dozens of thoughts.

Jose looked more dejected than we did.

No use throwing down the bags. We just climbed back in the truck and bounced and jerked over the same road bumps we had practically memorized by now. Our favorite desk clerk back at the Hotel de Turistas almost cracked a smile as he checked us into our same messy rooms we had just bid a thankful "good riddance."

What now?

I immediately told the clerk to try to get us a telephone line out if it takes all day, with the most urgent and threatening look I had used so far. I passed a few Intis toward him. He took them, then picked up the phone, listened, looked up and shrugged. "posible, mas tarde."

We had to trust that he would keep trying. He now had two strong incentives to wake up, a threat and a bribe.

Guillermo and I had to wait. Jose waited with us. The thought of our currency transactions crossed my mind again. It had been weird. I remember that I had exchanged only $200. After buying that first dinner and giving Captain Victor about $150 worth of Intis, I had only about $50 worth of the stuff left. Oh, well, we still had some dollars to exchange, and credit cards were good in Lima.

I had asked Jose if there was any change available from the original money after they purchased provisions and he had said yes, but never gave me any. I asked again a couple of days later and received the same answer, but no change. Now it was clear to me what had happened. Fearis had told us it was appropriate to tip the guides after the trip. When I forked over the 550,000 Intis, they had purchased a few things like rice and bread, maybe those Brazil nuts. Not much, really. No doubt they had thought the balance was a tip. After all, the twelve gallons of bottled water I had ordered was nothing more than one used plastic jug of tap water, or worse. We had eaten mostly fish we had caught, citrus we picked, and some of my peanut butter.

Furthermore, when the Inti was established not long ago to replace their overinflated Sol, it was worth $.37 U.S. Inflation in the international banking system now had it worth about two tenths of a cent. Seems crazy.

Well, in this rainforest, far from Lima, far from any international banking, far from any import and export markets, the Inti was just a medium of exchange that would buy whatever it would buy. In Puerto Maldonado, for instance, if Juan sold his eggs to Chico for 4 Intis per dozen and then, two weeks later, Juan wanted a 4 Inti sack of flour from Chico's store, would Chico say, "So sorry, Juan, but the London currency exchange says that the Inti has been devalued by 75% and you have to kick in some more Intis?" Of course not. This town was not affected by the vagaries of daily exchange rates, or even the Lima values, except in the long run.

"Bill, did you notice that only Jose has seen us since we have hit shore? Where is Captain Victor?"

"Yeah, his clothes ought to be dry by now, that little a******. Wonder why he never even showed at all. Where does he live, I wonder?"

"Bill, I think we made him a millionaire in buying power here in the jungle. Not kidding. If we can get a motel room for peanuts and buy a dinner for four for $3.75 worth of Intis, that would normally cost us at least 50 to 100 bucks anywhere else, that would make the Intis we gave him about four to five thousand dollars' worth of actual buying power here. No wonder he never asked us for money to pay El Jefe's fee or anything else. He just took that as our gratuity. A nice tip. No wonder he never asked for any more-for anything. He's rich now. Why take a chance that we would ask for our change again?"

The funny thing is, we probably would have given him a tip like that anyway. This was still a very cheap trip...if we make it home someday.

After bearing down on our Zombie desk clerk, making him understand we were serious about getting a phone line out, he reminded us that it would be more like "generator hour' before he expected to get a line. "I told him 'Bullshit. It doesn't have anything to do with his generator, just stay on it." I wasn't sure I was right but I would try anything to get this lazy pile of nothing to stay with it. "Sigue intedando."

Adding to our frustration of having all our options slammed shut, there was fear. What might happen at home when we went missing? Again, we went uptown. I stuck my head into places with people and said, "Does anyone here speak English" and was usually met with a variety of cold stares or head shakes. This can't be. No roads or railroads out to anywhere. No water traffic. No telephone, telegraph, or radio. No airplane options other than to hope one comes and then, that we could board it. No horses, llamas, camels or any damn things but pecke-peckes to deeper jungle.

We never got a telephone line that day. We ate some forgettable crap for dinner. I made notes, wondering if I would ever be able to use them. This time we had fairly dry clothes, so we didn't unpack anything more than Dopp kits, and hit the sack.

Chapter 21

Ramos, El Milagro

The next day we had no better plan than the one we had followed the day before. The ride to the airport was the same, but as we arrived, Jose began to yell, "Aeroplano esta aqui! Ha."

Sure enough, the airport building door was open and we could see an airplane on the ground outside, a Boeing 727. It looked enormous in this single runway jungle clearing that passed for an airport. We went in anyway.

More people crowded into the little building than we had ever seen. None looked like happy friends waiting for their first pleasure cruise of a lifetime. They seemed to be all native men, stocky, sweaty, smelly, pushy and busy. Behind the counter one weary man held up his hands. He yelled something, then ducked into a small enclosure with the door half falling off. Whatever he said caused some groans and some outcries. He was no longer available to the people at the counter. The door was shut. Surely, he was coming back. Jose was out of his element. No help.

The crowd compacted itself into a tight ball at the ticket counter, an agitated bunch of native men of all sizes and manner of work and old clothing, all pushing and yelling. A couple of them pounded clenched fists on the top of the counter. We had our duffels and bags by our side just standing in the back of the crowd. We had no idea where to take it from here. There was no queue, no apparent procedure, just a mob of natives pushing toward the counter and nobody behind it. We had far more luggage than anyone there.

We were completely blocked off from any chance to try for the airline ticket counter. Should we push it or pull it up through this crowd? Impossible. As they say in redneck, they looked like a big litter of piglets after a one-teated sow.

I suddenly noticed a gut-wrenching sight over the window of the small partitioned office behind the counter. It was a sign that read: AERO-PERU #432 CANCELADO

Our flight. Our hopes smashed. This town's only airline schedule called for Aero-Peru #431 from Lima to Cuzco and then to Puerto Maldonado and the same plane, then renumbered flight #432, returns to Cuzco and back to Lima. That was ours. Canceled.

Shit!

Hopeless again.

What was the other plane doing here? It wasn't Aero-Peru. It was white with red trim and said Faucett on the side. No telling what we should do or how to do it. There was turmoil all around us. I just stood there with our tickets in my hand, in a puddle of total frustration I had never experienced in all my travels anywhere, at any time.

I looked at Bill and saw he was tight-lipped and serious without anything to say. I said to him, "Bill, watch the luggage. I am going to try to get to someone." I moved to the left of the crowd at the counter, hoping to come in from the left, sliding along the counter in front of some, yelling in English. Maybe the airline person will take notice or something from hearing a different voice.

Some of the toughest, smelliest, thick-bodied natives were not about to give up their spot at the counter, pounding on it and yelling. I knew I was taking a chance. Pushing against these wild, strange natives might find me with a knife or a dart or maybe a fist stabbed at me. The mob was not happy and not civilized. I found my way back to Bill.

We discussed it and decided that we would stay in here until the mess was over, refuse to leave and haunt the airline people until we could talk to someone, or negotiate some way of getting out of here. Heat was coming out of both our collars. We might even have been close to doing something desperate and stupid, but this was a frustration unlike anything either of us had ever run into.

It was just then, as we stood there in our wrinkled and damp clothes, tickets in hand, duffels and bags at our feet, that a miracle happened. Looking back, even years afterward, we realize that the chances of this happening are more remote than Bill's double-eagle. Standing near us at the rear of the crowd, a complete stranger—a man in his forties dressed in a business shirt, more Latin looking than native—spoke to us in English with a Spanish accent, "Ees that your flight was canceled?"

I was so surprised to hear English that I was startled, "Well, it was the one we hoped to get."

"Why you don't take that airplane out there? That ees special flight to Cuzco and Lima."

"We would love to. How do we do that?"

"Ah, we see." He then grabbed my tickets and immediately handed me his briefcase as a gesture of mutual trust. I quickly looked in his briefcase and could see at once that there were important belongings, real things no businessman would give up, like a passport, check book, etc., not gimmicks to pull off a scam and get our tickets. Besides, he had two young associates or helpers with him who stood next to us, holding his suitcase. All he took were our two—useless—pieces of paper tickets.

He abruptly left us and headed toward the counter. We stood there awestruck and hopeful as he attacked the rear of this mob. He physically brushed by people, moving them out of the way, talking as he pushed. Near the counter, he actually climbed over the backs of the pushing, noisy, angry mountain of people, stepping on a couple of them. We stood there, mesmerized. When finished with his assault on the summit, he stood on top of the ticket counter. He then jumped down on the other side, yanked open the one hinged, partitioned office door and disappeared inside.

Minutes went by. The crowd was still anxious. The next time we saw him he was actually standing on the counter waving to his two helpers to pass up the luggage—his and ours.

People either didn't know what to make of it or accepted him as an official of some kind. His movements, his dress and demeanor appeared authoritative, confident and forceful—like someone in charge. Anyone who could stand on the counter yelling orders without being pulled down by an airline official had to be in charge.

His name, we discovered, was Jose Luis Ramos—a travel agent from Lima, with some sort of business here. He never revealed why he was in this Maldonado Port. Probably, to these people, many of whom had never even seen the inside of an airplane (or even one in the sky), a "travel agent" might easily be considered an official. To us he was a miracle, our milagro.

Miraculously orchestrated by Ramos while standing on the ticket counter, our duffels and his things were passed over the crowds of surly natives and onto the counter. Ramos, our rescuer, then dropped them down on the other side, tagged them and put them out a small door where someone would load them on a dolly and to the plane, we hoped. We think that the crowd let this all occur without protest, thinking that this man was at least going to make some things happen. Nothing else was happening.

Ramos jumped down, made his way back to us and signaled for us to follow him out a door that was not the one used to load passengers. Everything chugged along fast now. Bill and I kept pace, which meant a little rougher shoving through the people than was comfortable. I wouldn't have been surprised if someone had taken a swat at me.

Ramos was the leader. I was physically as large as most in the crowd; Bill towered over everyone in the building; and we looked foreign, which might have helped. There was certainly nothing regal about our rain-beaten clothes. We weren't going to let any opportunity slip by. Following Ramos out a door onto what might be loosely called the tarmac, we were not stopped by any of the armed and uniformed personnel, so we were in the open, out on the runway area.

People clutching their tickets left the building and stood in the line to board the plane. The plane was from Faucett Airlines, an old Peruvian airline that had made a special unscheduled flight here, probably in order to fill up a planeload and collect fares from the canceled Aero-Peru flights.

Several uniformed men with rifles slung from their shoulders watched us patiently. They looked just as confused as any of the hapless, hopeful passengers. They just seemed to look on, doing nothing and hoping to continue to do so.

Ramos said people were forming two lines, one for those going to Cuzco and another for those to Lima. "Follow me!" He led us on a path away from the lines, around behind the building and out toward the plane, approaching it from the rear, under the wing. We found ourselves approaching the passenger line from the side, not far from the man at the foot of the ramp who was checking passengers' tickets before allowing them to enter the long stairway ramp to the plane. We were actually cutting in. The Lima passengers were boarding first; the Cuzco passengers were holding, and that line was longer.

With a quick gesture to Bill and me to follow him, Ramos led us quickly and directly to the head of the line where the airline official was checking tickets of Lima passengers who were about to climb the portable ramp to the plane.

Ramos stopped, boldly held his hand out in a gesture to hold back the boarding passengers, slipped us into the line as if we were all important, and handed the man the tickets for the three of us, with his on top. Apparently, his two helpers were locals and not coming.

Ramos was headed for Lima. He sort of pushed us to go up the ramp at once, ahead of him, as he handed over the tickets. The ticket taker took a look and shouted something to Ramos as we were partway up the ramp. He had apparently seen that our tickets were for Cuzco, not Lima. Ramos quickly told us, "Stay here! Stay here. No move."

We froze there on the portable staircase, about a third of the way up to the plane, gripping the low railings to keep from being nudged over the side as several Lima-bound passengers squeezed past us and climbed the steps. Then, with a couple of words from the ticket checker, Ramos, now the last Lima passenger, proceeded past us and told us to follow.

Bill and I then became the first Cuzco passengers to board, a perfect move. We were almost the last to get inside this packed Boeing 727 sardine can, leaving a few still on the ramp and an angry crowd of thirty or forty people still in the line on the ground, expecting to board this plane.

There was no galley on this plane, no first-class section, just the maximum number of minimally-sized passenger seats they could jam in right up to the lavatory and flight attendant seats. Loading and seating in this plane started in the rear and moved forward. Since we were nearly last to board, Bill and I sat in the front two seats directly across from the open door and a view of the ramp. Ramos had found an aisle seat a few rows behind us.

The plane was now full. A few people still remained on the ramp and many more still in the line below. The waiting crowd got louder. A pilot came out to gesture to them to go away. In our seats across from the open door we could see everything— the ramp, the crowd and the line of those who were not going to be able to board, and the guards with their rifles slung over their shoulders.

The door was not shut yet, and we could see that a fight broke out amongst the angry people on the ground who had not been able to board. They were getting louder. It wasn't just shouting anymore, it was screaming. A group of men grabbed the portable loading ramp and rolled it back from the plane with an airline employee and three would-be passengers still on it, all clutching the handrail for dear life. Then the angry crowd pushed it toward the plane, increasing the speed, and rammed it, shaking the whole craft. We felt the impact as our seats lurched. Noise broke out all over the plane. Angrier still, they rolled it back and repeated the maneuver to ram the plane even harder.

This was sheer destructive anger. The plane was full. No more passengers would make it aboard, no matter how enraged they became.

As we looked down, Bill saw one of the guards actually hit a surly native with the butt of his gun. That was like pouring gasoline on a fire—more pushing and shouting, louder noise.

We were shocked by the total inaction of the other armed guards. They just stood as if dumbfounded, paralyzed with fear and surprise, their minds in neutral, their rifles slung over their shoulders with their homemade slings like useless, decorative serapes. They didn't know what to do. Or were they part of it? Or sympathizers? Inaction at a riot certainly couldn't have been part of their training.

Nothing was done to stop the frenzy. It was disconcerting. No, it was terrifying. For a fleeting moment between impacts, I wondered if this was a possible hi-jacking attempt by the deadly communist insurgency, Shining Path. If they couldn't get control of the plane, were they intent on sabotaging it? They looked like a tattered mob from a hideaway, not your average business or vacation group, although none of the angry mob had actually pulled a weapon yet. That kept alive the hope that we still had a chance to leave.

The protestors rammed the plane again. We were now worried that these jolts could cause some damage to the landing gear or the hull that might put this plane out of service. I couldn't believe this was happening. A plane ramming? Since we were sitting behind the cockpit at the forward door opening where the ramp was impacting, we felt it the most, and, worse, we could see it coming. They were pulling it back faster and farther for even another ramming.

The perspiring pilot emerged and helped the nervous, wide-eyed attendant close the door. Satisfied, he took a deep breath, returned to the cockpit and immediately started the engines.

Roaring jet engines, up close, have a way of chasing people to look for cover. For anyone who has never experienced this roar without ear protection, it is lightning and thunder. The pilot revved it up loudly. Angry people scattered, holding their ears and ducking in pain.

That was a scene we never expected to see in our lives. Bill and I were a pair of shaken but happy, sopping wet escapees as we heard a beautiful sound—the plane's air conditioner blowing into the passenger compartment from overhead.

Air conditioning! It had been a long time.

We looked at each other with a tired smile and took a deep breath that said, Finally, finally on our way out of here. Clothes crinkled and clammy, this veteran gringo twosome was surely now headed for the ancient Inca capital, a hotel with hot water, some good food and, maybe, even a bottle of wine.

The plane revved its jets again and wheeled around to taxi back to the start of this single runway. It was a long, bumpy ride. We then turned for takeoff, engines in full power, and had just started to taxi down the runway when a passenger, out of his seat, came screaming down the aisle yelling, "Gasolina! Gasolina! Gasolina!" He pointed frantically at the windows. What now? Sabotage? Oh shit! Did some raving native shoot at our tank?

Already gaining speed for takeoff, the engines were killed and we stopped. Now what? This never happens.

"Bill, do you get the feeling that they don't want us to leave?"

Disgustedly and soberly, Bill mumbled a familiar expletive from our collection, which I can no longer recall. I seconded.

We had visions of either being unloaded and taken prisoner or spending another night in the 0.3-star, cold water, dusty, musty, smelly, rat- and roach-haven Hotel de Turistas. Never thought I would ever find myself hoping for the latter.

The pilot came out of the cockpit and down the aisle to see what the panic- stricken passenger was yelling about. What he saw was this little red-faced man crying and pointing to the windows where we could see some trickles of liquid streaking down the outside windows. He must have thought there was a leaking fuel tank above the windows. It was just the normal accumulation of moisture on this aircraft while it sat in the jungle, sweating. As we started to speed up, it just blew loose and poured down over the windows.

We figured it was his first plane ride and he was scared, or was it?

More than a little disgusted by now, the pilot turned around, mumbled some angry words, went back to the cockpit, slammed the door and moved the plane back to the start of the runway again. We took off, leaving a cloud of red dust to cover the angry protestors.

I would have given a week's salary to hear what the pilot said as we at last cleared the final trees and climbed into the sky.

Once in the air, Bill and I grinned at each other's bearded faces and took a good, long look at the top of the vast jungle canopy we had been living under for a very long time. One could not help noticing how bright things were above the canopy in contrast to the hushed darkness under it. We sat back to take ample time and really sort out and enjoy the complex maneuver and the fast action that Ramos the Miracle pulled off to get us on this plane. Although we had no way of ever knowing how he got away with jumping the counter and getting us ticketed, we did enjoy figuring out his moves on the ground to get us on the plane. We knew also he was understandably quite proud of it himself.

That one move of crowding us into the line of Lima passengers had already put us ahead of the waiting Cuzco passengers. Then putting his ticket on top of ours and sending us up the ramp without bothering to wait for approval placed us halfway up the narrow stairs to the plane when the ticket agent finally noticed that we were bound for Cuzco.

With so many in the line already in a panic-loading mode, it was easier just to leave us there. When it was time for the Cuzco people to load, there we were, first in line. Ramos knew the agent would not want to take the time and trouble to return us to the end of the Cuzco line. Besides, wasn't Ramos a pseudo authority figure directing two important foreign people on board?

The ticket taker wisely realized that it was no time to double-check credentials. A potential riot was brewing and speed was important. He wanted to get this thing over with as soon as possible.

From Faucett's point of view, the fares to Lima were obviously greater revenue than the shorter hop to Cuzco. Cuzco passengers were taken on only as empty-seat fillers. As it turned out, only the two of us and a couple other Cuzco passengers made it. The plane was full, and the crowd below was explosive.

We knew we were more than just lucky. There was no way we could have gotten on this plane without Ramos and exactly the actions he pulled off. Running into him was the greatest stroke of luck imaginable. If this plane had served drinks, we would have toasted him.

This plane served nothing. It was a bus, a human cattle car. To us, though, it was a golden carriage with a team of white horses.

In our first relaxed and celebratory way, we gabbed about ways to thank this man, our savior. Bill suggested giving him a free pecke-pecke cruise to the Bolivian pampas with Victor and Peckahead. Naw, maybe something else, like a dinner for four at the Danubio Azul Restaurant in beautiful downtown Puerto Maldonado with unlimited cocktails. Of course, we could also consider an all-expense-paid roundtrip ticket in Jose's rickshaw and an hour at the Velasquez Bordello Barn. Or an evening of both.

We agreed that, in actuality, we probably owed him a new Mercedes, but we finally agreed to look him up when we reached Lima in a couple days and treat him to a great evening. Maybe we could think of something authentic by then to express our gratitude.

At that moment we were a pair of malodorous, unshaven gringos, highly skilled at truck bed and pecke-pecke riding, worn-out explorers, escaping in a worn-out airplane somewhere over a jungle in South America—but happier than two kids in a swimming pool.

Chapter 22

Incas, then Conquistadores,
now Guillermo and Company

As euphoric as we were after escaping our imprisonment in that jungle town, and as much as we wanted to see the mountain peaks and sights as the plane climbed up the Andes and over the first snow-covered cordillera, the cool dry air of the cabin and fatigue put us in the deep snores in minutes. We dreamt of cool, dry air, a hot shower, an icy drink and an actual bed. We didn't wake up until our Faucett pilot bounced us into the Cuzco airport.

Had we known more about this airline, started by Elmer Faucett years before, we may not have had the nice snooze we enjoyed. This was one of only two 727s owned by Faucett. Later this same year, 1990, Faucett crashed this very plane in the Atlantic Ocean off Newfoundland. Then in 1996, they crashed their other one in Peru, which was the worst airline crash in the country's history. Better known for their accidents than anything else, Faucett Airline folded in 1996.

Once inside the building at Cuzco, we made sure to find an English-speaking agent to secure our tickets onward to Lima in a couple days and then to Miami and Chicago. It wasn't easy, but a lot easier than leaving Puerto Maldonado.

Our luggage arrived in no worse condition than the same dirty, wet condition it was in when Ramos checked it, so we grabbed a black taxi and made our way to the Hotel Libertador. We booked two rooms for two nights and then made our arrangements for tomorrow's trip on the narrow-gauge railway train to Machu Picchu.

The air in Cuzco's high mountain valley was thin, dry, and mosquito-free, completely different from the heavy closeness of the jungle. It was no wonder the Incas chose this for their capital city. Once we were checked in and had deposited our luggage, we grabbed a couple of our nearly moldy garments— the ones we wanted for travel—and left them at the desk for the hotel laundry to struggle with. It was still early in the day, so we spent the rest of the afternoon with Juan de Dios, a driver with a great name, who was furnished by the hotel desk clerk. Juan, like our guides Victor and Jose before him, spoke no English. But we were used to that.

Cuzco is full of colorful people. They seem to like red. We looked at their adobe architecture and the ancient Inca structures with their mammoth stone walls built with giant carved rocks of granite, fitted perfectly together. One rock may have as many as twelve sides, touching twelve different adjacent rocks, each with its own shape but all touching all abutting rocks perfectly without gaps. Giant granite jigsaw puzzles. The masonry skills and the technique for fitting, lifting, and moving these gigantic rocks are still not fully understood.

A note for anyone reading this: In Quechuan, the native language used by the Inca Empire, words are spelled five or six different ways depending on whether it is phonetic Spanish, English, Portuguese or something else and by what dictionary.

(Like the spelling of the city itself: Cusco, Cuzco, Kuzko or Qosqo). I hereby direct any reader to accept any spelling I use as correct by at least one of the authoritative references—please.

Not a lot is known either about the Inca Empire's history before the Spaniards' arrival, due to their lack of a written language. Without reading and writing, one wonders what the first and second grade Inca kids did in class. They did use a system of record keeping known as "quipu," which is a series of strings and knots denoting mathematics and possibly words. But this, like their masonry skills, still hasn't been well deciphered.

That's not all the Incas didn't have. They didn't have the wheel, nor did any of the indigenous cultures in the "New World" of North and South America. Of course, a wheel by itself would be useless without the invention of the axle to support a load and the ability not to wobble. Furthermore, they possessed no horses or beasts of burden to pull a wheeled vehicle. South America is home only to llamas, alpacas and vicunas, and they aren't strong enough or willing. The Inca roads were steep, not flat, and used stairs a lot. They also did not have the invention of gunpowder, steel or the arch. They did use a trapezoid for some of their bridging stonework.

The Andean women we saw in Cuzco wore very colorful dress consisting of alpaca wool in layers of unmatched patterns in various shades of red. Shallow baskets (monteras) were perched on their heads, tied with a cloth around their chins. They may be empty, filled, or decorated with almost anything they had lying around that day, maybe even lunch. Hand-woven baskets were used to carry things. The Incans were good at all kinds of weaving, including ropes, carpets and textiles of all patterns and textures.

A number of young people tried to sell us jewelry they had made from stringing together distorted coins. They wanted an amount equal to fifty cents or a dollar for necklaces, so we each bought a couple of them. Later we realized that we should have bought dozens. This activity, of course, drew a horde of peddlers out of their usual siesta hiding places.

Because the climate is normally cool or cold in the mountains, the women typically wear wide skirts (polleras) and big square things like carpets on their backs, called llicilla. (Pronounce that one. Remember that ll is pronounced like y in English.) These were the descendants of the Incas, once considered to be the largest single native culture in the Americas.

At one farmhouse a man had a giant Andean condor tethered in front of his shed. It is the largest flying bird in the world. We could hardly believe our eyes. It is primarily a vulture with a gigantic appetite. The owner prodded it in a way that made it spread its wings to their full span, which was over ten feet. Its wings were thick, its talons long and it looked as if it could carry off a goat or a kindergartener. He said it was just a young one, probably close to full size but not yet covered in all its mature coloration and feathers. Our non-English speaking Juan couldn't tell us what it ate while it was in captivity. It looked as if it could have devoured a burro.

Juan took us out of town to a place called Saksaywaman, an ancient Incan fortress above the city, consisting of a series of terraced walls made of giant stones. It is at an elevation of 12,000 feet but is part of the city. We were told that the Spaniards took much of the original stonework to build their buildings in Cuzco. The longest wall in the fort was over 1,000 feet.

We returned to the hotel, where my partner, Guillermo the Gringo, and I bought bottles of some kind of red wine before retreating to our rooms for a long-anticipated shower with genuine clean, clear, hot water. The shower stall itself was a vision of heaven and couldn't have been better. It was roomy, had a big showerhead and a smooth, bare hardwood slat bench to sit on. Very comfortable.

Holding my glass of red wine, I sat on that welcomed bench with a near-orgasmic flow of hot water pouring over me, turning the temperature up one notch every minute. I probably drained the hotel's tank. I sat there in ecstasy for at least an hour, thinking about how great it felt not to be standing in cold muddy water, slowly sinking into the mud nearly knee deep and dumping a bucket of cold, tortilla-colored river mud over my head while wondering if one of those little flesh-eaters would get curious about the splashing, mistake it for a dinner call and rip off a toe. Well, it may have been longer than an hour.

I vowed right then to never again take hot water for granted.

Bill and I met later, relaxed and withered from marinating in the steamy shower, and had a real dinner in a real restaurant and talked about what to take with us to Machu Picchu in the morning. According to the desk information, the day might be rainy. That wasn't too bothersome since the clothes we would be wearing were downpour veterans, still rumpled and ready for more. We were sure any inhabitants of the ghost city wouldn't care.

It boggles the mind to think that for all those thousands of years of human cultural, commercial, political and scientific advancements and exploration by all the empires of Europe and Asia, explorers never learned of the existence of the massive continents of North and South America and the people who lived there until the 16th century CE. Even though the Vikings touched part of North America earlier, inland exploration was minimal.

It took that Genoan navigator, Christoforo Colombo, or Cristobol Colon (who had been seeking financial backing from several countries to let him test the theory of the earth's global shape), to finally convince King Ferdinand and Queen Isabella of Castile to sponsor his sailing west to arrive in the Orient. Most calculations at that time indicated that the known curvature would make the trip too long, and they were correct, except that

Columbus ran into this new, unknown world of the Americas and their islands. For the next century and a half, it was the Spanish conquistadores who fanned out their exploration, touched many lands in the New World, claimed the land for Spain, subjugated or killed the poorly armed natives, stole their gold and silver and forced them to adopt Spain's language and religion.

The largest native empire in this continent was that of the Incas, which was a federation of many tribes stretching from today's Colombia to northern Chile, entirely in the Andes mountains, not on the coast or in the Amazon valley. It was estimated to consist of eighteen million natives. They had adopted a common Incan language (Quechua) and had about 700 local tongues. There was an administration and some trade. Transportation consisted of walking, with llama and alpaca to carry some loads.

Spanish conquistadores were revered at home and often were granted governorships of these newly claimed islands and countries by the Spanish king. Francisco Pizzaro, who had been with Vasco Nunez de Balboa in 1502 when he discovered the Pacific Ocean, returned on other trips of his own in 1523 to attempt to conquer the Inca emperor.

He returned to Spain with enough Inca gold to earn a governorship of Peru in the North along with a partner, Diego DiAmalgro, for the South. On his next voyage to the area, with his brother, sixty-two cavalrymen, 100 well-armed infantry and, of course, the ubiquitous Catholic church officials, he sailed south along the Pacific coast in some ships that had been assembled in Panama. With him was an officer named Hernando DeSoto, whom he sent inland to find the Inca capital and emperor named Atahualpa. DeSoto returned with the news that the emperor had just finished a victorious civil war against his brother and was resting near the city of Cajamarca.

Since Pizzaro's second cousin, Hernan Cortez, had been so successful in Mexico by going straight to the Emperor, Moctezuma, capturing him and ruling in his name, then killing him, Pizarro would try the same with the Inca emperor. He arranged a meeting with the emperor in the town and set up an ambush, capturing Atahualpa and killing his personal guards and hundreds (or thousands) of Incans with the Spaniards' superior weapons.

The Incas were obviously awestruck when the first soldiers showed up mounted on these giant animals they had never seen, covered in the finest Toledo steel armor, carrying long halberds—spear-like battle axes—plus steel swords, sharp enough on both edges to decapitate the enemy soldiers. The Incas felt terror when the soldiers rolled up those dreaded harquebus guns that belched thunder and killed at long distances. The Incas had only wood lances, clubs, some bows and arrows and slings, none of which was a serious problem for armored, highly-trained Spanish cavalry and infantry.

This "battle" of Cajamarca was a slaughter of Incans by 180 Spanish marauders.

The emperor was captured, transported to his capital of Cuzco and held for ransom. In four months, the Incans filled the room in which he was held with gold, then two more rooms with silver. This ransom was estimated to be over eleven tons of gold; it was melted down and gradually shipped to Spain. Not satisfied after a few months, Pizarro had Atahualpa tried (by Spaniards), found guilty of plotting to overthrow the Spanish, rejecting the bible and Christianity, and for murdering his own brother. He was given a choice of burning or being strangled. The story is that he chose strangulation in order to preserve his body for the afterlife. The Spaniards strangled him in a public spectacle.

I imagine that one could see a lot of that gold decorating the Cathedrals in Spain.

Pizarro then took the emperor's wife and a few dozen others. Of course, the Spanish version also includes the story that the emperor was handed a bible and threw it aside, rejecting Christianity. During this time of the Spanish Inquisition, a deed or word against either the church or the king would cost you your life. It can be a convenient way of eliminating rivals (or justifying a murder?). It cost Balboa and many thousands of others their lives during that time. Ironically, it happened that it was Pizzaro who was given the dubious honor of decapitating Balboa.

For many years to come, taking land, treasures and women from these heathen natives became standard operating procedure for the European takeover of this New World. It seems that committing these crimes in the name of the crown and Christianity, then building a mission in the town, made it acceptable and justifiable—if one can digest the irony and hypocrisy of it all.

The struggle for power could often backfire also, since Pizzaro actually had his partner, DiAlmagro, killed. Then to even the bloody score, he, himself, was later assassinated by DiAlmagro's son in 1542, in Lima, a city Pizzaro had founded.

Hernando DeSoto went on to explore North America on his own years later and gained some fame when he discovered the Mississippi River. He died of fever in Louisiana at about the same time Pizarro was killed in Peru. For nearly 300 years, Spain and Portugal controlled the islands and continents in this new world from north Florida to the tip of Chile. The area was known as "New Spain."

All this history made our next day's visit even more interesting since it seems that the mountain peak city of Machu Picchu was actually abandoned and lost to both the Incans and Spanish until discovered by an American historian in 1911.

Chapter 23

Mysterious Lost City of Machu Picchu

W e boarded the small train from Cuzco's station in the rain. The train goes only to Machu Picchu and back. It starts from Cuzco's Station as a switchback, chugging uphill for a way, stopping and reversing as it switches tracks and backs up another, and so on, about five times—until it is high enough to clear the city's rim of mountains. It then switches to the long downhill track to Machu Picchu, going from over 12,000 ft. down to 8,000 ft. at destination. The trip took about three hours, with the first part of it paralleling the violent, tumbling, splashing Pomatales tributary downhill to the big Urubamba River, which cut the deep canyon around the peaks upon which rests this strange, deserted city of Machu Picchu.

We paralleled the river, enjoying the jungle view out the rain-streaked windows until the train stopped at a platform near the bottom of the canyon, across the river from the narrow, zigzag road that climbed up to the ruins. We crossed a bridge, then took a strange and scary-looking vintage bus that strained as it pulled up the rain-soaked winding road to the top. This bus had a short wheelbase, making the rear end hang far out beyond the rear wheels. We were seated in the rear, and sharp turns actually swung us out over the edge of the precipices.

"Don't look down, Bill." So, of course, he immediately did.

"Oh shit!" one of us said, "let's go sit up front." But we didn't move, just toughed it out.

There seemed to be about a hundred hairpin turns and we cringed on every one, praying that we weren't too tail heavy. When the wheels slipped on the slick, muddy pavement, so did our stomachs.

As we reached the upper level and the entrance to the ruins, I remembered, again, another fun note our "trip planner" gave us in case we ever made it to Machu Picchu:

Look for the checker named Juan (baggage check at the entrance to the ruins). He'll show you the Vizcacha (small animal that looks like a squirrel/rabbit/rodent) at the right-hand side of the ruins down at the jungle edge on the rocks at 5:00pm each day. Give him enclosed note. (He'll love a tip. $2 is plenty). If he shows you the animals. Good luck, Barbara.

There was no Juan, it was raining, I didn't have the note, we weren't going to stay until 5:00 and besides, a vizcacha is just a long-tailed rabbit or a fat squirrel with long ears (viewer's choice.)

It rained all day. We put on our ponchos, walked around a little, saw what we could of the terraces for agriculture, the rooms, the temple of the sun, the sacrificial rock and all the stone masonry that will probably last for eternity. There weren't roofs on anything except a couple of caretaker rooms. The city was much larger than I imagined and was no casually constructed native village. A masterpiece of organization and planning, it must have taken years and thousands of workers to build. It sits on a peak with very steep granite cliffs, and sits in a saddle between two taller rock points. Virtually impenetrable.

Terraced gardens were built for their agriculture. Their engineering skills were obvious in the technique of building hillside terraced agricultural gardens with their layered soil and rock, drainage and heat retention structure allowing them to grow food during cold periods. These structures also indicated a knowledge of astronomy, a religion and governess. How could this cloistered tribe have been self-sufficient on this remote mountain ridge?

Hiram Bingham, the American historian, discovered it in 1911 and named it Machu Picchu (old peak). It might have been mistaken for the secret city where the Inca rulers fled when the Spanish ruled. Some Incas actually did establish a shadow empire in a place called Vilcabamba, not far from there to the northwest. Lately, Machu Picchu is thought to have been a retreat for the aristocracy of Incas. Parts of it are estimated to be hundreds of years older than the Incan empire, and that fact only adds to the mystery. (The suffix bamba keeps popping up, attaching itself to a lot of names. It means valley.)

The city seems to have been lost to both the Incas and the new Spanish rulers. It is also possible that it might have been a special place of worship and housed the most beautiful and revered women, possibly a religious retreat. Seventy-five percent of the skeletons found there have been women.

Could Machu Picchu have been a grandiose Inca version of Velasquez's jungle bordello barn?

"Hammer, take some photos while we are here," Bill asked me. He had me take a lot of really not great photos of us all over the city so we could look at them someday over a cup of coffee. I did, and we looked more like store mannequins posed in some stonewall setting, featuring a two-for-one sale of cheap blue ponchos.

That afternoon we returned to the train and a much longer ride back up the 4,000 feet of altitude to the switchback tracks at the valley of Cuzco. After another slow and salubrious hot shower, a meal of some mystery fish, a corn paste concoction, all washed down with a dark red imitation of wine, we packed up for the morning flight to Lima and finally home. I'm certain we both slept with smiles on our faces.

Tomorrow we would have time enough between flights to look up our rescuer, Jose Luis Ramos, and pile on some more gratitude.

Chapter 24

A Great Last Day

The scratchy buzz of the hotel's wake-up call was so annoying that it kind of made me homesick for the jungle alarm chickens. At least chickens were trying to sing. A quick look in the mirror showed a bearded, sunburned, worn-out explorer with no more red spots with white centers. They disappeared as mysteriously as they appeared. With a couple of bags, our duffels and a couple of handfuls of bows and arrows, we met in the lobby, settled the bill and grabbed a taxi to the airport. Checking in, we discovered the airline would give us boarding passes and check our luggage only as far as Lima. We would have to check in again that night for the Eastern Airlines flight to Miami. That was just as well, as we would have more control of our luggage.

In checking bags, however, we were in trouble carrying bows and arrows. Airline agents said that they considered them armas mortales—deadly weapons—not allowed on board aircraft. Obviously, the security hombres had never seen my marksmanship. They were too long for a suitcase or duffel bag. We finally handed them to the checker, who wrapped and tagged them, and we retrieved them in Lima.

Once in that sprawling city of Lima, founded by Pizzaro himself, we called Ramos, our miracle "Salvador de los Viajeros." He picked us up at the airport. What a welcome sight he was.

We took him to lunch at a restaurant of his choice, which became a special experience on its own. A driver took us to a place called playa de Mireflores, a beach on the Pacific Ocean. It sported a long pier reaching out into the ocean about two hundred yards, ending at a bridge leading to a large Victorian-style restaurant on pilings right out there in the Pacific Ocean, defying the big swells that come from the far reaches of the sea. It was named La Rosa Nautica and provided a spectacular 360-degree view of the ocean and the shoreline of the city. The walkway on the pier was made of hardwood planks in a herringbone pattern with railings and ornate shelters of latticework along the way. Roses grew in planters at each shelter.

The restaurant is elevated enough to allow the great Pacific swells to roll under it on their way to the beach. Diners can see the waves coming, pass under the restaurant and watch from the rear as they crash on the beach. While we were there, surfers appeared to come from the sea and travel near or under the restaurant. The venue is noted for having sensational sunset views. We could have spent hours there, just watching the sea. It was much like being on a ship without being tossed about by the waves.

After our long lunch and discussion of Ramos' life and business, he arranged for a car and an English-speaking driver to take us around Lima and then to the airport. We visited some of Lima's fine shops and one unforgettable museum. The museo, "Oro del Peru" is a collection of a Peruvian billionaire, Manuel Mujica Gallo, a builder and banker with a lust for history and artifacts. The displays were not fancy or well organized but the Inca gold (apparently not melted down by Pizarro), and historical light arms from Peru and Europe were mind-boggling. His collection included, allegedly, Pizarro's sword, Napoleon's pistols, Hitler's and Goering's knives and cabinets of gold pre-Columbian art, mummies from Ecuador and many more artifacts that would mesmerize any historian.

In fact, some artifacts piled in the corners of this crowded few rooms would be centerpieces in many other museums. I could have spent a week in there, and have often thought about going back to Peru just to visit that building.

We shopped a little before our driver delivered us to the airport as the sun dropped into the Pacific. We checked in, checked our mangled, muddy luggage and our "deadly weapons," and climbed aboard our soon-to-become-extinct Eastern Airlines aircraft heading north. We agreed that we were happier, wiser, slimmer, and grateful for this absurd trip we would never forget and our even more memorable great escape.

No matter how many decades, gray hair and safaris later, Guillermo and I continue to enjoy recalling this trip. We are glad we went and realize how lucky we were to come through it in two pieces.

The trip was far from perfect, fraught with unknowns, but the natural environment of this vast rainforest in Amazonia is one of the earth's least explored but most important and prolific resources for life on this planet. We feel fortunate to have seen some of it in its undisturbed state. We can only hope that the human development that is sure to come will be done with care and preservation.

Although I still like Brazil nuts, forest land and jaguars, I am totally weaned off of piranha fillets, boiled mud water, bats, electric eels and two-man tents.

I will never again take for granted a hot shower or an iced drink.

End

Postscript

My partner, Guillermo, is not only the easiest travel companion one can imagine, his trip-planning experience, now tempered by fire, came to the finest edge in our next trip he planned. It was a perfectly flawless game-viewing safari in the Serengeti. An exciting, entertainment-filled, well-managed itinerary that I can say was the greatest trip I have ever taken.

We hope you thoroughly enjoyed reading Lee Flandreau's *NO WAY OUT* and we would like to encourage you to check out the other titles available from BluewaterPress LLC on the website at https://www.bluewaterpress.com.

www.ingramcontent.com/pod-product-compliance
Lightning Source LLC
Chambersburg PA
CBHW060319030426
42336CB00011B/1120